Praise for *Star Brands*

"These days everything and everyone bills itself as a brand—from sodas to athletes, to, if they could (and if they existed), unicorns—but true brands, those that become integral parts of our lives, are cast from years, if not decades, of vested nurturing and leadership from a key group of people behind the scenes: brand managers. A great product, service, or personality without the proper guidance will simply simmer mildly without the potential of becoming what Rogoll describes as a "Star Brand." This book provides a tangible framework to aim for that lofty status through clearly explained processes and milestones that both new and seasoned brand managers will benefit from implementing on behalf of the brand they've been entrusted with."
~ **Armin Vit, co-founder of UnderConsideration**

"Trying to jumpstart your career in brand management, but can't decide between entering a top business school program or learning on-the-job from a successful experienced marketer? Do both . . . by reading this book."
~ **Paul Smith, bestselling author of** *Lead with a Story* **and** *Parenting with a Story*

"Next time I get a tricky question from one of my clients, I might say, 'Wait, let me check page X of *Star Brands*,' as the book cuts all the corners and goes straight to the point on how to build a big brand."
~ **Renata Florio, global group creative director, Ogilvy & Mather**

"A startup cannot afford to wait to work on their brand until they are successful. Instead, the Brand Experience must be an integral part of how an entrepreneur approaches their company from day 1. In her book, Carolina gives entrepreneurs an insider view of how to apply the principles of brand building so their companies will be positioned to one day be a Star Brand."
~ **Dave Knox, co-founder, The Brandery**

"In an attention economy, brands need to unlock their star power to ensure relevance and value exchange with the people most likely to purchase their products. The old playbooks for brand-building need updating and Carolina provides a refreshing framework for brand managers to build brands in today's marketplace."
~ **Sarah Hofstetter, CEO, 360i**

"I thoroughly enjoyed reading *Star Brands*. Even after thity-six years in the world of branding, I learned something new. *Star Brands* is written by someone who loves branding, thoroughly cares about her reader, and knows from her unique perspective as a practicing brand manager and as a teacher how to demystify brands for businesspeople, students, and even professionals looking to distinguish themselves in a competitive marketplace . . . Carolina's unique combination of loving brands and loving to teach the subject is impressive."
~ **Jacquelyn A. Ottman, author,** *The New Rules of Green Marketing: Strategies, Tools and Insights for Sustainable Branding*

"One of the great pleasures of reading *Star Brands* is how authentically it reflects Carolina's voice and the experience of working with her on the day to day challenges of building a great brand. Carolina has encapsulated her years of experience into a practical and fun guide to the process of marketing, from analyzing the lay of the land to defining a vision; developing and executing a plan; to measuring results and continuously feeding learning back into the marketing plan. She takes complex ideas and distills them to their essence, illustrates them with clear and easy to understand examples and then links them so that you clearly see the impact of each decision and how everything should work together. Whether you are new to marketing, a seasoned marketer who needs to mentor others or work on the agency side and want a fresh perspective on how a client approaches branding, *Star Brands* is a smart, pragmatic and empowering guide to marketing today."
~ **Alain Groenendaal, president and CEO, Grey Latin America**

"Having always found the study of branding—and the relationship we as humans have with brands—fascinating, it was an extremely rewarding experience to attend Carolina Rogoll's Brand Management seminar. The unique star brand model she teaches, presented in this book, allowed myself and my fellow students to better understand how the processes of building a brand happen, and then also to apply them to real life cases. Not only do I better understand the discipline of branding more deeply, but also feel better equipped to build and manage any brand."
~ **Olivia Barry, SVA Masters in Branding Alum, Class of 2014**

"In an age of posts, likes, and tweets, we focus all too often on short term thinking and instant results. Carolina's book presents a timely reminder that great brands and great businesses are built by people who can see the bigger picture and plan for the long term. Better still–she explains how to do it . . ."
~ **Julian Boulding, president, thenetworkone**

Star
Brands

A Brand Manager's Guide to
Build, Manage & Market Brands

Carolina Rogoll

with a foreword by Debbie Millman

ALLWORTH PRESS
NEW YORK

SVA
NYC

Published by Allworth Press, an imprint of Skyhorse Publishing, Inc. 307 West 36th Street, 11th Floor, New York, NY 10018. Allworth Press is a registered trademark of Skyhorse Publishing, Inc., a Delaware corporation.

www.allworth.com

Cover and interior design by Myles Gaythwaite

Library of Congress Cataloging-in-Publication Data is available on file.

Print ISBN: 978-1-62153-463-1
Ebook ISBN: 978-1-62153-474-7

Printed in China.

The author, Carolina Rogoll, is an employee of the Procter & Gamble Company. However, the views and information in this book are solely the author's and are not intended to represent the views of Procter & Gamble. Neither Procter & Gamble nor any brand discussed in this book have sponsored or endorsed the book.

buildstarbrands.com | carolinarogoll.com

With deep gratitude to all my mentors
who added fuel to my spark

Table of Contents

Foreword   *xi*
Introduction   *xiii*

Chapter 1: Star Brands   *1*
Chapter 2: The Leaders Behind Star Brands   *11*

Step 1—Brand Assessment and Goal Setting
Chapter 3: Brand and Market Assessment   *21*
Chapter 4: Vision and Goal Setting   *39*

Step 2—Defining Brand Equity and Target
Chapter 5: Defining Brand Equity   *59*
Chapter 6: Selecting a Brand Target   *81*

Step 3—Crafting a Communication Strategy
Chapter 7: Insights, Benefits & Ideas   *109*
Chapter 8: Understanding Media   *137*

Step 4—Establishing the Marketing Strategy
Chapter 9: Marketing Strategy & Mix   *165*
Chapter 10: Selecting the Marketing Mix   *175*

Step 5—Building the Marketing Plan and Measurement
Chapter 11: Marketing Plan   *189*
Chapter 12: Measurement Plan   *203*

Acknowledgements   *223*
Glossary   *224*
Notes & Index *231*

Foreword
By Debbie Millman

Marshall McLuhan and Quentin Fiore opened their 1967 book *The Medium is the Massage* with the image of a logo "printed" on a raw egg. Before the success of perennial brand darlings such as Nike, Starbucks, or Apple, McLuhan and Fiore commented on the "colonization of attention through the inscription of surfaces," or the notion that logos would begin to appear on anything and everything. The caption on the yolk read, "A trademark is printed on a raw egg yolk by a no-contact, no pressure printing technique. Imagine the possibilities to which this device will give birth!" In 2015, we no longer need to imagine. Today we have brands on bananas. On basketballs and on a young man's shaved head. Opportunities of every type—on coffee cups, in public bathroom stalls, on clothes, in marathon races, on diapers, in newspapers, political campaign posters, in philanthropy and even on wedding invitations—they have all become landscapes in which we can insert an impression of our brand affiliations. This inscription is no longer enough to capture the attention and the affection of an audience.

Brands have become cultural transitional objects, and they now have the unique ability to both differentiate ourselves from others as well as fit in with those we seek to differentiate from. With brands we assert our beliefs, we telegraph our allegiances, we project out how we want others to view us. We choose brands that make us feel most socially confident and we wear these badges as personal signifiers . . . whether it is deodorant, coffee, water, shoes, or handbags. Virtually no brand is exempt from this cultural communication and at no time in our history as a species on this planet have we asked more of the brands in our lives.

Why do people love some brands and not others? Why are some brands more successful than others? Why do people feel deeply connected to some brands and deeply dislike others? Ultimately, brands do more than differentiate categorically— brands also differentiate attitudinally. Now consumers choose brands that make them feel most socially confident and wear this badge of cultural acceptability . . . whether it be soda, sneakers, douche, condoms, cigarettes, beer, or mouthwash. As a result, we have entered a day and age where the notion of brand is an extension of human facility, whether it is psychic or psychological. Brands now create magical worlds inhabitants can understand, and where they can be somebody and feel as if they belong. We can now join any number of tribes in any number of ways and feel part of something bigger than who we are on our own. In 2015, consumers don't just "get" brands. Brands also "get" people. And people like brands the most when they feel they fulfill their needs and "get" them.

In *Star Brands: A Brand Manager's Guide to Build, Manage & Market Brands,* author Carolina Rogoll provides a unique framework in understanding how this magic actually happens. In her position as both a brand manager at the world's largest consumer goods company and as an educator in the world's first graduate program in branding, Rogoll is uniquely qualified to reveal the wizardry behind the curtain and, in doing so, she bestows upon her reader the very tools necessary to grasp this elusive but ultimately attainable creative business process.

Carolina does this by outlining her proprietary five-step framework aptly titled the "Star Brand Model." This model provides practical information and structured guidance to build and manage any brand. Carolina clearly and cleverly communicates how her framework applies to many of the global brands leaders in the market today, and she accomplishes all of this while leveraging her decade of experience actually working on the frontlines of brand building (after all, she is practicing what she preaches).

Contemporary culture is now almost entirely composed of brands, and I contend that the condition of brand reflects the condition of our culture. As Carolina writes in chapter six, everything we consume—even the most basic commodities like water and salt—are brands that satisfy needs. Experiences are brands. People are brands. Our role models are people, and thus our role models have become brands. Brands are so persuasive in their personal, political, economic, aesthetic, psychological, moral, ethical, and social consequences that they leave no part of us untouched, unaffected, and unaltered. Any knowledge of culture is impossible now without an understanding of the implications of "brand." Fortunately for us, Carolina Rogoll fundamentally and unequivocally understands the living and working context of these implications. Her Star Brand Model can be applied to any brand, in any stage of its development, at any size and in any market, and in doing so, she shows how to honestly and authentically create meaning and momentum.

Introduction

I've been chasing Star Brands, those that shine above the rest, since an early age. When I was seven years old, I began collecting stickers and candy covers that had bold colors, interesting fonts, and distinctive shapes. I carefully selected and organized them in beautiful binders with translucent paper similar to stamp collector books. It was my private, curated collection of brands. By the time I was ten years old, I discovered the connection between branded products, marketing, and money. I started my first holiday business going after a very actionable target: households with extra cash in my neighborhood. I sold Christmas lanterns that I would carefully select at the wholesale market my mom would take me to. I realized I could sell them for almost twice the price to my neighborhood target. I rapidly expanded into offering a line extension, my self-made holiday cards that I would design myself. I knew differentiation and a touch of personalization were important so I talked to a local calligrapher to create some templates that I could use. I sold many holiday cards.

And so I went on my journey on playing with brands, with my sporadic business ideas: jewelry from Czech Republic, revamped paintings upgraded by placing them in nicer and colorful frames, and so on. I did this for a couple years, but my businesses really never took off as a sustainable brand. I didn't really have a consistent or organized approach on how to grow my product lines or how to differentiate them. I was being too transactional. I also wasn't really making much money and didn't know how to manage these businesses as brands. I decided that I was better off focusing on my studies so I could graduate and learn how to build brands at a real company some day.

I began studying business administration. After completing my studies to earn this and another degree in marketing and management, I was hired by Procter & Gamble (P&G), the world's largest consumer goods company and the "Mecca of Brand Management," prior to graduating from college. I was in heaven. I remember talking to my favorite marketing teacher about landing a job at P&G and him telling me, "Carolina, this is amazing. You will be playing and learning how to grow brands and even getting paid for it." I knew at that moment that my love affair with the art and profession of building brands had formally begun. It seemed like it was the job I was preparing myself for since I was seven years old. That is how I got started in my profession of learning how to build Star Brands.

Fast forward to today. After studying the best Star Brands for over a decade, I learned how to build these brands. I've been privileged to successfully build, manage, and market a billion dollar brand. Passionate about building capability, I've been teaching what I believe has made these brands successful for a couple of years too. Star Brands prove best the marketing, theory, and brand management practices that work.

Now, in this book I've summarized my brand-building experience in the form of an easy-to-follow, step-by-step approachable framework for your benefit as well.

The Star Brand Model is my personal take on an ideal brand-building process. It's a compilation of over a decade of experience building brands at the front lines of a big multi-national company and the soundest theory I've encountered in my research, marketing, and business studies—from business administration to the traditional MBA. I've also had the opportunity to personally interview many brand-building minds from active chaired professors at top international business schools to Chief Marketing Officers. The Star Brand Model has been curated with experience of real brand management practitioners as well as top-notch academic theory.

In this book I will take you through the Star Brand Model, a five-step framework that provides practical information and structured guidance to build and manage a brand, just like brand managers do. You will learn how to assess the brand's unique challenge to get crystal clear on what your brand stands for, who it should target, how to craft a solid brand strategy for growth behind a solid marketing mix, and then measure your success once in market. The Star Brand Model can be applied to any brand, existing in any stage, from a brand merely on the brink of conception to one with a strong, rich history.

This book has two audiences. One is the graduate level student from my Brand Management class. The other, any professional or startup that wants to learn how to successfully build a brand in a very practical way. I want to simplify the existing brand management theory for students and professionals and make it more actionable with a touch of reality. I suspect that most active professionals are not able to sign up to do a two-year MBA, navigate a dense MBA text book on their own, or shadow a real brand manager to learn about brand management. Meeting the needs of these readers was my main motivation in creating this book.

As a professional brand builder, it is my personal wish that you benefit from a strong theoretical yet practical foundation like the Star Brand Model to build any kind of brand. As business people and marketers, I believe we have the responsibility to create better brands and products that truly fulfill peoples' most desired needs. To do so we need to understand the theory and follow a disciplined process to building brands that meet the needs of the people we market to. This is my contribution to you, the future brand builder.

May you use the Star Brand Model to successfully build, manage, and market brands. Let's get started and good luck!

1

Star Brands

"Tell me your name and your favorite brand."

I ask my students this same question every year on the first day of my class in the Master's in Branding program at the School of Visual Arts. One by one, they begin raising their hands, introducing themselves and sharing their favorite brands. Some seem very excited to associate themselves with a brand, while others are far more reticent, trying to decide on just one.

I've taught this class for several years now, and I continue to be amazed at the consistency of the brands that the students name as their favorite. As you might well imagine, brands such as Coca Cola, Apple, Starbucks, and Nike all make repeat appearances, as do regional fashion favorites and popular "green" brands.

For some students, the enthusiastic supporters, a favorite brand is more than a simple product preference; it is a statement of character. In some way, large or small, the brand has qualities they identify with, the same qualities that they want others to see in them. They love these brands and are proud to be associated with them.

The passion these students exhibit for their favorite brand is the gold standard for measuring a brand's success. Brands that are able to connect with the hearts and minds of their customers are brands that will thrive. Beyond providing unique and functional benefits, these brands have built relationships with their customers over many years, fostering emotional ties and creating long-term brand loyalty.

The brands that do this consistently year after year, the ones that my students continue to raise their hands for are what I call Star Brands. They are the celebrities of the branding world, the leading lights that we all look to in admiration, and sometimes, a little awe.

Brands don't become stars overnight. Star Brands are a result of many smart and assertive brand choices backed up by a strong and successful business model. Building them requires careful planning and thoughtful execution consistently over many years. The people responsible for building Star Brands have mastered the balance of brand love and business fundamentals. Star Brands are not only loved, they are profitable.

That said, not all Star Brands are the same. Each possesses a unique set of cultures and business practices; for example, no one would ever mistake IBM for Ben & Jerry's. However, for all of their uniqueness, I do believe that all Star Brands possess certain core qualities, in varying degrees, which are:

Core Qualities of Star Brands

- Clarity
- Consistency
- Higher Order Purpose
- Emotional Connections
- Superior Benefits
- Commitment to Learning

McDonald's has historically been very clear about what it sells and to whom.

Clarity

The Ancient Greek maxim of "Know Thyself" speaks to the importance of individual self-awareness and knowledge. This maxim also applies to brands. Star Brands know who they are. They know what drives their success, what limited them in the past, as well as how to grow and thrive in the future. This includes understanding their customers' needs, the insights to connect with them, and the right marketing mix for effective communication. When a brand knows what it stands for and whom it is trying to delight, it can execute its communication plan and product offering with excellence.

Consistency

Star Brands have consistent and recognizable branding and communication. Consistency in communication requires discipline. A brand experience is defined by "touch points," all of the points at which your brand's product or service touches the consumer. Star Brands surround consumers with total brand experiences that not only surprise and delight them, but also look, feel, sound, and smell how the brand intends, consistently, regardless of the touch point.

Consistency pays out. Frequent exposure to the same brand identity and message helps increase brand recognition and awareness. If you have a well-defined and managed brand identity combined with messaging that is compelling and executed consistently, your media investment will also have higher returns and go further in building the strength of your brand. Every time you make a change to your brand message or identity, you will have to retrain your consumer to recognize it. In other words, you must rebuild your consumer's brain to associate these new images and emotions with your brand.

"A Coke is a Coke and no amount of money can get you a better Coke . . . all the Cokes are the same and all the Cokes are good" - Andy Warhol

Higher Order Purpose

People like people who think like they do, and if given a choice, they will flock to a brand that supports their same ideology. According to a study conducted by research agency Millward Brown and Jim Stengel, former Global Marketing Officer of Procter & Gamble, having a higher order purpose or ideal that the company seeks to contribute to the world was the single most important denominator across the fifty fastest growing brands from 2000–2010.

For the brands studied, their purpose was the core driver of strategy, innovation, decisions, and behavior. Star Brands are intentional with their purpose and aspire to deliver on a higher meaning beyond the product or service they sell. Therefore, it is very common that in the process of reaching stardom, great brands become more intentional about their purpose and actively communicate it.

Since its inception, Yvon Chouinard has committed Patagonia to be a valuable resource for environmental activism & advocacy.

Emotional Connections

Brand relationships are like human relationships; we become acquainted, we try their goods or services, we decide whether we like them or not, and then we begin to have, or not have, a longer and deeper relationship. Star Brands develop long and meaningful relationships with their customers, and they do this in part by establishing strong emotional connections.

Just as in human relationships, brands cannot, and should not, try to create strong emotional ties with everyone. However, once a relationship is formed, it should be treated with care and nurturing attention. Star Brands don't treat their customers like ATMs or simply as sources of profit. They see them as co-creators in the brand conversation, striving to meet their needs and satisfy their desires with verve and confidence.

Superior Benefits

The benefits a brand offers are what set it apart from its competition. The more distinctive the benefit, the more distinctive the brand, which will in turn attract the greatest number of customers. Benefits don't have to be purely functional. They can also be aesthetic, emotional, or stylistic. How or why a brand delivers a product can be an even more powerful driver of choice than how well that product performs; performance all too often becomes mere table stakes in the competitive arena. Star Brands focus on offering relevant and authentic superior benefits. They excel at delivering, communicating, and nurturing their most distinctive characteristics. This allows them to drive preference among the right set of consumers.

Commitment to Learning

A learning organization, a term first coined by MIT scientist Peter Senge, is one that facilitates the learning of its members to expand their thinking capacity, allowing them to better adapt to the changing market conditions and evolve over time[1]. Star Brands have systems in place to document their history and key lessons so they can be shared across the organization to help make better future decisions. They learn from the past and quickly adapt to the future.

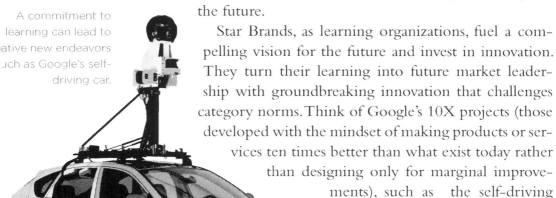

A commitment to learning can lead to ative new endeavors uch as Google's self-driving car.

Star Brands, as learning organizations, fuel a compelling vision for the future and invest in innovation. They turn their learning into future market leadership with groundbreaking innovation that challenges category norms. Think of Google's 10X projects (those developed with the mindset of making products or services ten times better than what exist today rather than designing only for marginal improvements), such as the self-driving car or the balloon that gives Internet access to remote areas. These ideas push the limit of imagination and technology to deliver on Google's purpose and go well beyond its main search engine product and current primary source of revenue.

Star Brands' relentless commitment to learning guarantees that they will never be stuck in time. If they learn faster than the competition, they will also always come out ahead. If Charles Darwin would apply his evolution theory to brands, he would talk about learning organizations: "It is not the strongest of the species that survives, nor the most intelligent that survives. It is the one that is the most adaptable to change."

THE STAR BRAND MODEL

In the realm of human achievement, the nature vs. nurture debate is long running and not likely to be settled anytime soon. However, brands aren't born, they're made, and while certain characteristics of a brand come about out of fortuitous circumstances, most successful brands are the result of following well-defined processes or frameworks.

A brand framework is not a formula, but a guided set of strategic choices that you can make on a consistent basis to increase the odds of achieving brand love from your customers. Over time, these choices are calibrated with failures to achieve strong and consistent market performance. Following a framework to build a brand is known as the brand-building process.

Successful brands often follow a disciplined and consistent brand-building approach. It's easier to accomplish a goal knowing which steps to follow than figuring it out randomly as you go or trying multiple things at once. Brand building is about creating differentiation in the market place — and communicating those differences effectively, to the right consumers, at the right time.

The Star Brand Model presented in this book is a simple yet powerful five-step process for building brands. My ultimate goal is to offer a strong foundation to those seeking to learn brand management principles to construct robust, effective and successful brands that deliver on a desired business goal. Following the Star Brand Model will not only help you inculcate the qualities of Star Brands within your organization, but it will provide a strategic outline for putting those qualities to work in the marketplace.

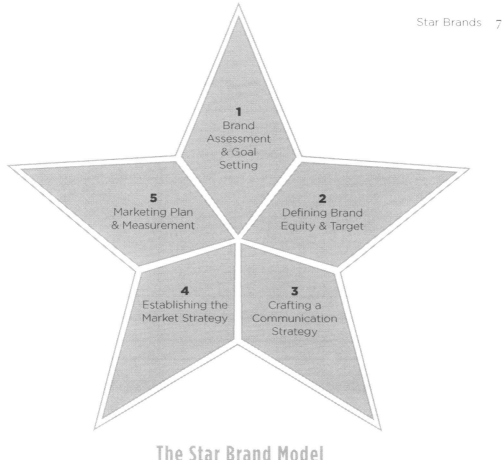

The Star Brand Model

The simple five step model for building powerful brands

The Star Brand Model is inspired by the lessons of what Star Brands do best, backed up with real-life brand management experience. It's a hands-on brand model written by someone who has been on the job for several years. Less theoretical and complex, the Star Brand Model is actionable and ready for you to use.

Using the Star Brand Model to build a brand will also help build the confidence of key stakeholders, including management, clients, and investors. Knowing there is an actionable plan with well-defined metrics gives stakeholders the confidence to take risks with you. This is true for existing companies determining budgetary allocations as well as start-ups looking for funding.

As a brand builder, you won't get all of the choices right or be able to control everything that happens to the brand. However, many brand choices are within your control and with the right attitude, a little bit of luck, and the Star Brand Model, you can build your brand successfully.

How to Use the Star Brand Model

Building a brand is a journey, so I will walk you through a series of steps, a process of discovery, strategy, creativity and action using the Star Brand Model. Following the steps in order will give you the greatest chance of success. If you are already well along in your brand journey, refining the earlier steps will ensure that you have based your strategic decisions on strong fundamentals.

Regardless of where you are in the brand-building process, each step will help you ask and find answers to important questions to further your progress. Answering these questions will give you and your team greater focus and help you make strong strategic decisions to bring your brand to market. Each step will include case studies and real and hypothetical examples to maximize your learning. There are five steps in the Star Brand Model. The first four focus on defining your brand and strategic goals, while the last focuses on building a plan to implement them in the marketplace.

Step 1—Brand Assessment and Goal Setting

In this step, you will learn how to define the market environment you will be operating in, including an assessment of the brand's core strengths and weaknesses via a SWOT analysis. The goal of this first step is to articulate the current status of your brand and to begin to chart your brand-building trajectory. Based on this starting point you will be able to formulate core business challenges and set a vision for your ultimate success.

Step 2—Defining Brand Equity and Target

This step is about defining what your brand stands for and to what group of consumers it most appeals. You will learn how to define your brand equity and select the target audience for whom your brand is most relevant. This step is based on the principle that what your brand offers—your Equity—and the type of audience you choose—your Target—are highly interdependent.

Step 3—Crafting a Communication Strategy

In this step, you will learn how to discover insights and benefits for your brand, and how to use these to generate new communication ideas. You will also learn how to write an advertising brief—the foundation for effective brand communication. I will also discuss the media world in general, as well as share enlightening case studies about credit cards, beauty products, and beer!

Step 4—Establishing the Marketing Strategy

In this step you will learn how to define the ideal marketing mix by understanding and selecting core components of your brand's marketing strategy. We will also learn how to quantify the impact this mix will have on potential sales and brand growth.

Step 5—Building the Marketing Plan and Measurement

This is the meatiest step of all and where the previous four steps culminate. You will learn how to bring all the elements together into a solid business plan with a well-defined marketing mix. The marketing plan will also include the defined core elements of your brand from the previous steps as well as go-to-market choices for your product or service such as pricing, distribution, and promotion, including communication and media. This step will also include a measurement plan for determining the success of your strategy in market.

You can use the Star Brand Model with any entity, product, brand, or person that you are looking to successfully transform over time. You can even use the Star Brand Model for your personal career development—helping to define your leadership or professional equity in the same way a brand would. After all, throughout your career you are looking to increase your market value and hone in on what sets you apart from other professionals. Just like a brand, having a clear, well-defined equity helps you determine where you want to work and which target companies might be interested in you. You have to break through the clutter in the marketplace when you are trying to build your career.

Ultimately, the Star Brand Model is about success—both for brands and individuals. Achieving success is a matter of defining: who you are, what you stand for, where you belong, and what to communicate—coupled with a solid action plan. Let's get started by first looking at the people behind Star Brands, and what they do to build them.

2

The Leaders
Behind Star Brands

Star Brands are the cumulative expression of an entire organization's efforts to shape and build a brand. This does not happen spontaneously, but through the coordinated efforts of men and women we call brand managers. They can exist at the executive level in large corporations, overseeing specific brands, or they can exist at the small business level, where brand manager is but one of the many hats a small business owner wears. Regardless of level, a brand manager is the person responsible for the development and execution of a brand strategy seeking to grow the brand's awareness, competitiveness, and value in the marketplace.

At its heart, this book is really about teaching you to be a better brand manager through the Star Brand Model. But before we dive into the model, I'd like to dedicate this chapter to what it means to lead a brand. Let's begin by taking a look at the origin of brand management, when the core principles were first put into place.

PRINCIPLES OF BRAND MANAGEMENT

Let's go back in time to the early 1930s to Cincinnati, Ohio, where a young Neil McElroy was struggling to survive in a tumultuous market. A promotions manager at Procter & Gamble (P&G), McElroy was frustrated by a lack of resources and manpower needed to properly promote the Camay soap brand he was supervising. Not only was he competing against brands from Palmolive and Unilever, but also against Ivory soap, another P&G brand. He became convinced that in order to succeed, he, and Camay, would need greater independence in the organization coupled with a singular focus on the brand.[1] On the morning of May 13, 1931 McElroy sat down and wrote a very compelling memo to his boss, P&G's president R. R. Deupree. Little did McElroy know that his memo would not only forever change the very structure of P&G, but would alter the entire consumer goods industry.

Over the course of three pages, McElroy laid out his plan of creating a concentrated task force of what he referred to as "brand men." His recommendation specifically stated that each brand should be assigned a dedicated team that would better manage all aspects of the brand and help each to become differentiated, something that didn't exist up to that day.

Not only did he receive additional resources and manpower, his "brand men" memo became the catalyst for P&G restructuring its business around brands and laid the groundwork for P&G's subsequent astronomical success. The McElroy memo forever changed how consumer goods companies would organize themselves. The brand management system shifted the focus of the company's operations by balancing centralized oversight with decentralized decision-making by brand groups, which would have unique knowledge and insight into a brand and the market forces surrounding it.[2]

What makes the McElroy memo so special, besides being the origin of brand management, is that a close read of the memo will reveal six principles of brand management that remain valid to this day: Analysis and Measurement, Executional Leadership, Accountability, Collaboration, Brand Advertising, and Operational Discipline[3]. A manager of Star Brands will need to master them all.

Analysis and Measurement

Brand managers are expected to have a pulse of their brand and the market at all times. McElroy makes the case for studying the "field", i.e. the market, as the primary means of analysis. In his memo he gave great detail on how to analyze market performance with personal investigation of retailers and consumers trends. He suggested that where the brand is performing well "examine carefully the combination of effort that seems to be clicking and try to apply this same treatment to other territories that are comparable." In short, understand the history of your brand's performance in the market, note what is working, and seek to apply that knowledge to analogous areas that are underperforming.

Executional Leadership

McElroy places the "brand man" as the leader of the brand. This includes leading the planning and execution of brand activities. This is why brand managers are often perceived as project managers, responsible for the coordination of a plan to move the brand toward its strategic goals.

Accountability

With leadership comes accountability. McElroy intentionally used the reference of "take full responsibility" when describing critical brand activities the "brand man" performs. He or she needs to assume complete responsibility for understanding brand strategy, advertising, budget, and ultimately, the market sales.

Collaboration

Even with the brand manager in the driver's seat, McElroy emphasized the importance of collaboration with subordinates and district and division-level sales managers. The "brand man" should obtain the district sales manager's authority and support for corrective action, as well as establishing ongoing communication and check-ins "a number of times a year to discuss with him any possible faults in our promotion plans." Strong interpersonal and communication skills are a must for any successful brand manager.

Brand Advertising

McElroy began his Procter & Gamble career in the advertising division. He was well aware of the demands of the advertising process, which included evaluating the ads or "printed words," and planning and budgeting for it. So he expected the "brand man" to be the one responsible for all brand advertising. Similarly, he expected the "brand man" to "experiment and recommend wrapper revisions" alluding to the importance of the brand's packaging and the brand managers's thought leadership needed in this area as well.

Operational Discipline

Finally, McElroy describes what might be the most important quality of a "brand man"—one who can instill discipline and rigor into the brand-building process and "follow through to the very finish to be sure that there is no let-down in sales operations of the plan," and "to be sure that the amount of money proposed can be expected to produce results at a reasonable cost per case." In other words, a "brand man" is someone who can make a plan and budget, execute that plan, and then measure the results for future action.

MODERN BRAND MANAGEMENT

While today's brand managers greatly benefit from following the original brand management principles from McElroy, their jobs have also become increasingly more complex in the last decade. The changing nature of today's consumers, the fragmentation of media, and the rise of digital technology have placed significantly new demands on today's brand managers.

Modern brand management is the intersection between growing the brand, business and people. So what traits do Star Brand managers need to cultivate to set them apart? I have posed this question many times to peers, mentors, executives, and recruiters. While their answers were not all the same, a core suite of characteristics began to emerge which paints a picture of a brand manager most likely to succeed.

Confident Business Leaders

They are visible leaders that are personally accountable for the vision and results of the brand. They make plans and remove barriers. They take the blame when things go wrong and are the calm amidst the storm. They motivate and encourage the team when times get tough and lead with both the heart and the mind. They are the role model of the team and possess the values they want the team to embody.

Set Stretching Goals and Deliver Them

They deliver exceptional results. They set stretching goals behind bold visions and guide the team to reach them. They have a keen understanding of the realities of the business, its strengths and weaknesses. Then they add hope to this reality and dream big about where the business can go if the team performs at its best. They communicate this vision clearly so they can drive it. They are determined to lead the team to victory.

Build the Brand with New Ideas

They create new ways to win the consumers' hearts and minds either with new products or new ways to connect with them. They champion and nurture big ideas. They are persistent in learning how ideas perform in the market and strive to continuously make them better.

Stay Open, Flexible and Curious

They recognize the need to be flexible and curious to keep up with today's consumer, market, and technology. In an "always on" world, we will need more "always on" brand managers[4]. They stay open to new ideas and different ways to do things. They never stop learning because they know they owe it to themselves, their team, and the brand they manage. They lead a learning organization.

Collaborate and Build Genuine Relationships Up, Down, and Across

They collaborate effectively at all levels. This includes upper management, other functional teams, and direct reports. They build strong external connections that can help pave a better future for their business and team. They take great personal interest in understanding what makes each person on their team tick. While collaborating, they persuade, bridge, or follow and swiftly adjust their leadership style as the circumstances require.

Behave Like a Coach and Publicist of Their Talent

They invest in their people with daily coaching and seek opportunities to stretch them. For their best people, they advertise their results, build them up, and look for opportunities to set them up for further growth—just like a professional publicist would do.

THE FUTURE OF BRAND MANAGEMENT

The qualities of exceptional brand managers will continue to evolve and change in the coming decades as markets evolve and consumer demands grow increasingly more sophisticated. To stay abreast of this ever-changing tide, I believe successful brands in the future will need to have even more mindful and thoughtful leaders at the helm.[5]

Star Brands of tomorrow will be more humane, more people-oriented. Brands are no longer dictating the terms of the market; they are part of a larger conversation where consumers and brands have equal voices. As such, future brand managers will become less transactional and serve more as connectors, recognizing that their job is about humans solving the needs of other humans via branded objects. They will manage their brands to deliver exceptional services, while delighting their customers and making greater contributions to the culture surrounding their business.

SUMMARY

In this chapter we discovered that skills such as analysis, executional leadership, and collaboration, brand advertising, and operational discipline illustrated by McElroy's Memo are still at the core of the brand management profession today.

Modern day challenges have pushed brand managers to be more well-rounded leaders that not only manage the business and brand well, but also their people. Traits such as confidence, bold vision, innovation, flexibility, learning aptitude, and high emotional intelligence, distinguish the strongest brand managers. These are the types of leaders behind Star Brands.

Now that you know what you need to bring to the table to become an exceptional brand manager, it's time to dive into the Star Brand Model and begin building exceptional brands!

Applying each concept from the Star Brand Model to a real brand will help you internalize the concepts better and realize the power of following a coordinated process for building a brand.

Starting now, I invite you to pretend and feel as if you are a real brand manager. I am your brand-building coach. You can choose any brand. If you are a student, pick the brand for your thesis or current project. If you are currently working on a brand, select that brand. You can also think of your favorite brand or even use yourself.

I am serious about you feeling like a real brand manager. In fact, I want to hire you as one right now. If you are ready to accept, sign your name below.

....

YOUR NAME

Is hereby hired to be the Brand Manager of

....

YOUR BRAND

Brand Assessment & Goal Setting

3

Brand & Market Assessment

"Know from whence you came. If you know whence you came, there are absolutely no limitations to where you can go."

–James Arthur Baldwin

Imagine visiting Disney World for the first time. You're super excited as you run into the park, but quickly shuffle to a halt, having become daunted by the endless possibilities. Where to go? What to see and do? Much to your relief, you soon find a giant map with the ubiquitous "You are here" locator. Breathing a sigh of relief, you devise a plan, note some reference points, pick a trajectory, and off you go.

Believe it or not, managing a business or brand is in many ways the same as visiting Disney World or a big park or city you've never been to before.

It's thrilling to think of all the possibilities that lie ahead, but before you can embark on your journey, it's important to understand where you are, what your current conditions are, and what surrounds you. Failing to understand where you stand as you begin your journey would, at best, make it difficult to reach your destination; at worst, you could waste your time running in circles, never achieving your goals. Only once you have thoroughly defined your current business environment and brand situation, can you begin to chart a course to your ultimate destination using the other aspects of the Star Brand Model.

So naturally, Step 1 of the Star Brand Model is assessing your current brand situation and environment. This assessment phase helps define your surroundings to determine which variables support growth, which ones inhibit it, and as a result which ones you need to actively manage to arrive to your ultimate goal.

The assessment process boils down to asking a series of questions about your brand and the environment in which it operates. Your answers to these questions will ultimately help to decide how to build, manage and market your brand.

There are two complimentary analyses that are important to conduct:

* **The Internal Assessment:** How internal stakeholders, people inside the organization, from the CEO down to hourly employees, or your business partners if you are a startup, currently perceive the brand.

* **The Market Assessment:** How the brand is perceived in relation to its competition in the marketplace as well as macro external factors.

These analyses are complementary to one another and together will give you the best assessment of where your brand stands, what your brand needs to begin doing, what it needs to stop doing, and what practices to continue. We will formalize and provide structure to these analyses with the SWOT analysis template—a tool that helps organize a brand's strengths, weaknesses, opportunities, and threats.

Before we begin, a note on terminology. When I refer to "brand" I am referring to more than logos, packaging, and advertising. "Brand" stands for the entirety of a particular business—its customers' experiences, physical assets, business model, employees, and other resources. Brand therefore is synonymous with business. Additionally, when I refer to "product" this could be either a physical product or service that a brand offers a consumer in order to meet a need. All concepts of the Star Brand Model are applicable to brands that sell products, services, or both.

INTERNAL ASSESSMENT

The first step in the brand assessment is gathering the point of view of the internal stakeholders. These stakeholders are people inside of the organization or close enough that care about the brand and are dedicated to its success. These can include employees, vendors, customers, investors, and the like. Gathering this information is done through a series of one-on-one interviews or team workshops that pose two simple questions:

* What is working for your brand and what should you continue doing?
* What is not working for your brand and what should you stop doing?

Using questions like "What's working?" or "What's not working?" and "What would you change?" is a great way to elicit passionate opinions about the brand from a broad range of stakeholders. Probing for both positive and negative views not only generates a more nuanced picture of the brand, but also helps the respondents to think more objectively, providing more open and honest responses.

Answers to the first question of "what's working?" will highlight areas of the brand that make people proud to be a part of it. You might learn about recent successes, particular strong contributions from individuals, or activities with proven and continuous market results. Be sure to probe a little deeper with follow-up questions to look for the historical drivers of a strong market performance. What individuals or processes are behind these positive outcomes? You need to come away with an understanding of the forces at work—is success a recent fluke in the market, or has it been sustained over time? Most brands' strengths are typically consistent.

The second question of "what's not working?" will highlight fissures in your brand, problems that could exponentially spiral out of control if not attended to. To dig deeper on problem areas, this question can also be followed with even more direct ones such as, "What would you change?" or, "If you were the leader of the brand what would you focus on?" These questions will likely get the most passionate answers. Asking someone what he or she would do if they were in charge will typically reveal their number one frustration: the one thing they feel should be immediately addressed. Asking these questions across a broad spectrum of stakeholders is a great way to gain a deeper understanding of the inner workings of your brand.

As the brand manager, you are the leader of the assessment process and will determine the best ways to conduct the analysis, consolidate key findings, and evaluate and digest information before making any final recommendations.

When conducting interviews or workshops, be sure to include representatives from every function within your organization including marketing, finance, sales, research, engineering, design, etc. The inclusion of myriad representatives from diverse departments will provide a more accurate assessment of where the brand stands. This will ultimately reduce the natural tendency of managers to minimize weaknesses and highlight strengths; or to be overly optimistic and less realistic when articulating brand-building opportunities. For instance, the profit/loss biases of a finance professional and the regulatory biases of a lawyer might best assess the downsides and risks of a situation. The consumer biases of marketing and external point of view of sales might best assess the upside potential. By asking the same questions about the brand across multiple disciplines, you begin to formulate a much more accurate picture of your brand's situation.

The internal assessment can be conducted in groups or as individual interviews. Both have their strengths and weakness. Interviews typically produce more honest answers, while a group exercise in a workshop format can help uncover communication issues or other team dynamics. In either case, it is important to not only sample a wide variety of disciplines, but a wide variety of positions and tenures as well—from the VP with ten years of experience all the way down to the new associate who's been there for six months. Those involved in the assessment will also be more likely to get personally involved to work on any interventions that come out from the exercises.

As the internal assessment is conducted, the feedback collected from the interviews and group exercise should be recorded in a way that it can easily be summarized, and compare responses to identify trends and common themes. As the brand manager, probe deeper on key themes that emerge to better understand their impact on the current business operations. What forces are at work behind the scenes? Digging deeper into problem areas allows defining the real magnitude of them and deciding if they are worth addressing.

Finally, you should also answer the questions from your specific point of view. This can be done prior to conducting the group assessment and again after completion to compare responses. Sometimes the first impression of looking at a situation with fresh eyes will be the most accurate. I always record my first impressions before embarking on an analysis and then validate my thinking with the complete assessment process and additional points of view.

The output of the internal assessment will be a consolidated list of the perceived health of the brand—elements of which the stakeholders believe are working or not working and what has to change vs. what should remain in place. You can also rank in order the issues based on their potential business impact to help further prioritize. This list will serve as a starting point of key areas the brand manager needs to focus on. To complete the whole picture, however, once the internal assessment is completed, the next step is to evaluate the brand vs. marketplace conditions.

THE MARKET ASSESSMENT

Where does your brand stand in the marketplace? How healthy is it compared with your competition? How is it perceived vs. your competition? The second component of the brand assessment consists in evaluating the key environmental forces that affect your brand, its overall health, and ability to do business. The forces that are identified in this assessment are the major factors that brand managers should actively manage.

Brand environments can be really complex. They include not only the already demanding world of consumers, media, and advertising—with their characteristic changes and expectations – but also the complexities of running the business itself which include variables such as operations, manufacturing, employees, government, and regulations.

Your brand's ability to succeed will be determined by its own health (both as a brand system and a financial enterprise) as well as consumers' preferences and behaviors in your particular industry. Let's study these factors in detail so you can assess them for your brand.

Brand Health

To determine the overall health of a brand you need to understand both its financial health, which is the lifeblood of its corporate existence, as well as the health of the brand equity as a system that has the ability to attract consumers to buy products.

Financial Health

There are many ways to determine brand health, but if your brand is not profitable, it will not remain long in the market. Financial health, defined as meeting and hopefully exceeding the expectations of your investors, is the cornerstone for understanding where your brand stands in the market. As a brand manager, you need to have deep understanding of the Profit and Loss statements of your brand. Where is your money coming from: Investors? Sales? And is it trending up or down? Equally important, how does this compare to the financial performance of your competition?

While financial health is the goal of any brand, knowing just how financially healthy your brand is will determine your options for future growth and change. How much capital do you have to invest in your brand? Is there room to invest in research and new business, or is it time to start cutting costs and focus on core fundamentals?

Brand Equity Health

As distinct from financial health, brand equity health seeks to define the overall uniqueness and perception of all the components of a brand such as strategy, communication, visual identity, and products that are set in place to create value in the marketplace. When a brand has a healthy equity it means that it is perceived as providing strong value to consumers, especially in relation to other brands that it competes against. Healthy brands are those that stand out; consumers are aware of what they stand for and have positive emotions towards them. As a result, consumers are allured to buy into the brand's products and be loyal to them over time.

To determine the brand's equity health, large companies will typically hire market researchers to conduct extensive studies to determine the strength of these factors. However, small brands can conduct similar research by doing field studies and interviewing current and potential customers. There are many ways of conducting this research. Be creative, but strive to honestly answer the following questions:

* How strong is the love of your brand? How many people would miss the brand if it went away forever?

* How is your brand tapping into your customers' hearts and minds? Do you understand them? Are you fulfilling their needs? Is your brand offering superior value vs. your competition? How does it compare on pricing? Is the pricing justified?

* Is your brand's offering unique? Does your brand offer superior benefits? If so, does the market recognize this?

* Does your brand have advocates? How about haters? How is your brand perceived online?

Conduct interviews, send out surveys, read online reviews! Strive to paint a picture of how current and potential customers might perceive the brand.

Market Trends

Simply put, market trends affect a brand's ability to succeed. Typically, the trends that have the greatest impact on a brand's success are: consumer, technology, and industry. Understanding each, where they are headed, and how your brand relates to them will greatly impact your success.

Consumer

Without customers there is no business. So any market trends that affect consumers will directly affect how a brand performs in market. For example, birth and mortality rate of a particular group of the population, changes in category perception, or a shift in habits are all socio-cultural and demographic trends that impact the number of consumers available in a category and thus a brand's future sales potential. These variables have the ability to grow or reduce the market size for the category and the number of available and interested consumers to buy into a brand propositioning. When assessing the brand determine how well you understand your consumer target and if you are going after the right one to deliver your long-term goals. Ponder whether the brand is riding the right consumer trend.

Technology

The environment variable that has affected marketing and consumer trends the most in recent years is technology. The rapid advancement of technology experienced in areas such as telecommunications has impacted the way newer generations, especially Millennials, connect with each other, perceive the world, and consume media. This is the first time that marketers need to reach a young adult population that went though their complete school education with access to computers and the Internet. The digitally-native consumers are inevitably wired differently than previous generations. In general, consumers have become empowered with technology and are more demanding, consuming media on their own terms, finding products without going to stores, and filtering out advertising more easily.

The digital revolution in media has forever changed how marketers allocate their dollars to other mediums beyond the traditional television and print. The immanent rise of digital platforms is forcing marketers to quickly expand their toolbox with new skills like real time marketing, social media, mobile, and content marketing so they can effectively reach consumers in these mediums as well.

Technology is also making ideas and products more accessible, allowing businesses to expand beyond geographic boundaries overnight. Availability and speed of communications has created an expanding global platform where brands have an ever-growing reach. This creates opportunities for brands that ride the wave and a threat for those that are become obsolete by not catching up with current times. Given the magnitude of the change technology is bringing to brands, it is important to determine in the brand assessment how technology is affecting your brand and how it is currently capitalizing on it. Articulate and assess how much and how well technology is being used by your consumers, by your product, your business operations, and people in your organization.

Industry Specific
Brand managers are expected to become experts in the product or services they manage which includes a thorough understanding of the industry norms and standard practices that need to be met in order to succeed. Specific industry trends concerning variables such as the legal and policy landscape, innovation, and retail dynamics can significantly affect how a brand conducts business.

Changes in legal regulation in specific categories can limit or expand the brand's ability to reach consumers. How the product is manufactured and how business is conducted impacts the brand's cost structure and its ability to make profits. Similarly, any new innovation that redefines how consumers perceive the category or changes how they use the product or service can be game changing for a brand's go-to-market strategy. If the competition introduces an innovation that is well received by consumers, the future of brands that don't keep up will be threatened.

Finally, any changes in the retail environment, such as retailer consolidation and rise of e-commerce, have the ability to affect the brand's distribution model and thus its ability to reach the consumer base necessary to generate sales.

Brands need to be ahead of the curve and truly understand the current and future trends dictating how consumers shop for the products they sell. As part of your assessment, consider specific industry trends that have the ability to impact the trajectory of your brand both positively and negatively.

THE SWOT

The SWOT will help you complete the market analysis for your brand. This approach is based on a detailed analysis of internal forces of your brand environment in the form of strengths (S) and weaknesses (W) and external forces that represent opportunities (O) and threats (T) in your growth trajectory.

How to Build a SWOT

The first step in building a SWOT is to define your brand's competitive set. Brands don't compete in a vacuum and the advantages or disadvantages your brand has over its closest competition will dictate how well it operates in the market—which is why market assessments are always conducted in relation to a brand's competition.

For our purposes, competition is defined as those products or services that could easily replace what your brand is offering. For example, take brands playing in the transportation arena. Could a bicycle brand be a competitor to a car company? If the car company's core product is high-performance automobiles, then maybe not; but if the car company focuses on small cars for the urban commuter, perhaps it could. The competitive set for a specific brand will then depend on how the brand defines the market and its market positioning.

Begin by creating a long list of every brand that could replace yours, within a specific market arena, no matter how farfetched. Next, reduce the list of competitors to top brands—those that have significant market share and distribution. You can also further narrow the list down by eliminating brands that you do not directly compete with. For instance, Ford would not concern itself with Ferrari, unless it was interested in breaking into the high performance sports car market. The more specifically you can define your market and competition the better, but don't be afraid to do multiple SWOTs if you find you have a range of competitors across multiple markets or if you have a portfolio of brands in the same category.

The SWOT Analysis

A tool for capturing your brand analysis according to internal and external factors

With your list of competitors and your assessments of market forces and trends completed, you can begin to populate the SWOT. The SWOT has four quadrants: Strengths, Weaknesses, Opportunities, and Threats. Here is what each quadrant of the SWOT overview should capture:

Strengths

Strengths are internal factors that offer a brand a competitive edge. Strengths can come from core branding elements, organizational processes, products, technologies, and human resources. The strength of these factors are measured against competition and become characteristics that set a brand apart from other choices in market.

Weaknesses

Weaknesses are internal factors that could stop or slow down a brand's growth and success. These are the brand's significant disadvantage against the competition. Similar to strengths, weaknesses can include core elements of the brand, processes, products, technologies, and human resources.

Examples of strengths:

* Strong brand equity
* Brand's market share leadership
* Superior performing products/ services
* Proven innovation processes
* Valuable organizational qualities, e.g., agility, low cost leader
* Distribution and supply chain
* Unique expertise or proprietary technology

Examples of weaknesses:

* Poor brand equity
* Low market share
* No brand loyalty
* Parity products
* Significant value gap vs. competition
* Lack of innovation
* Weak teams, e.g., lack of employee experience or low morale
* Poor product performance
* Inefficient company processes and procedures

Opportunities

Opportunities are external factors the brand can capitalize on to grow the business. These can be new trends that develop in market or big ideas the brand hasn't tapped into yet to activate. They can also be market opportunities that the brand uniquely owns vs. the competition if action is taken in the short term.

Threats

Threats are external factors that might affect the brand in the near or long-term future—changing market conditions that make it harder for the brand to compete or that affect the category and industry in general. A threat could also be a competitor building a significant market advantage in a short period of time.

Examples of opportunities:

* Growing market or category
* Increased consumer spending
* Improved positive sentiment towards the category
* Large market penetration opportunity consumer perception that favors the brand
* Fast-growing market segments
* Weak or slow-to-react competition
* Legal changes that uplift business barriers, e.g., global expansion or taxes

Examples of threats:

* Category commoditization, e.g., more consumers buying private label products Change in consumer habits that makes the brand's products less appealing
* Change in consumer perception that favors competition
* Competitor introduces a new proprietary technology
* Changes in distribution channels
* Government policy changes that affect product production
* Taxation rules which reduce the company's revenue or consumer income

The SWOT will be a useful tool for organizing the key findings and variables of your market assessment. Whether this assessment is conducted as a team or independently after surveying the team, each quadrant should be fleshed out starting from the internal forces: strengths in upper left quadrant to weaknesses in the upper right quadrant. Then moving to the external forces: opportunities in the bottom left quadrant and threats in the bottom right quadrant.

To avoid having a laundry list of items in each quadrant, once populated, the variables can be prioritized based on their importance and ability to articulate best the current state of the brand. Looking at the relative number and quality of the strengths, weaknesses, and the potential opportunities and threats will give you an idea of how strong your brand currently is, what might be holding it back, and which external forces could play a defining role in the brand's future.

BRAND EVOLUTION STAGES

The final step in the brand assessment is to understand the current "evolutionary stage" of your brand, which will help determine its future trajectory and change. Over their life span, brands pass through different evolutionary stages based on specific market circumstances and the growth strategy pursued. In the brand's assessment you need to determine the brand's current evolution stage and its previous trajectory to decide what to do next.

A brand's evolution doesn't necessarily mean it is moving into a more positive stage; it simply implies change and transformation. Some trajectories will look like a roller coaster, sometimes up and down, but all in all a steady upward trend. Other trajectories might feel like an uphill climb, for others a downhill drop or a flat line. It really depends on the magnitude of the change in market conditions. If the brand and market conditions are positive, the brand will have momentum to keep growing and play to win. If the brand and market conditions are uncertain or stagnant, so will be the course of the business. Finally if the conditions are negative, the business can begin to erode its market value and if not managed properly begin to free-fall or implode.

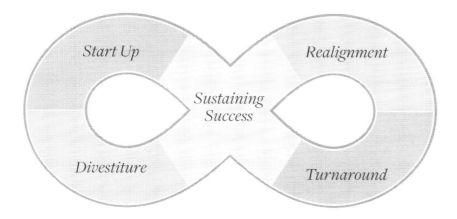

Brand Evolution Stages

Understanding your brand's current trajectory will help you select the right growth and brand building strategy

Each evolutionary stage the brand is in will create a new set of challenges, and thus requiring a different brand-building strategy. It will be your job as the brand manager to accurately assess the current business conditions and challenges and set the marketing strategy that will place the brand into a growth trajectory.

The five most common brand evolution stages are: Startup, Sustaining Success, Realignment, Turnaround, and Divestiture.[1] One brand can go successfully through all of them, stay in one stage for a long time, or never get past the turnaround stage. Some stages signal an upward trend, others a downward trend. A big factor on determining whether the brand stays in one stage or another is the vision and growth strategy that the brand manager pursues. You will learn how to craft that strategy in the upcoming chapters.

I've articulated what each of the evolution stages of a brand might feel like and the challenges and opportunities the leader behind it will face. The articulation of each stage will help you diagnose which situation your brand is likely to be in. Read the articulation and try to pair up your current situation with one of them. It's ok if you can't match the current situation to one of them exactly. The overall intent is to determine if the brand is on an upward or downward trend to help you select the appropriate growth strategy and approach to managing the brand.

Startup (upward)

You are getting your branded product or service off the ground. You are new in the industry or breaking new ground. The organization is young and growth can come from many unexpected places. You have a young team, probably few people with tenure. The environment is new for you, so the business course is less predictable. The brand is still fragile and being defined. Only a few customers are starting to buy the product or service you sell, some like it, some don't or are indifferent.

Brand building for startups tends to focus on identifying a differentiation strategy and a growth target. The most natural first consumer target for a start up is its current buyers – the first group of loyal customers. Organizationally, a startup leader needs to motivate by communicating his or her vision but also be able to recognize when to pivot their idea or stay the course. At this time, the brand manager will be obsessed with getting the business off the ground and will be also required to spend time building confidence among stakeholders and attracting additional investors.

Sustaining Success (upward)

You are a successful brand manager—outstanding business results, solid brand—and your team is strong and happy. Your challenge is how to keep it going without being complacent. By now you should have decoded your brand's growth model so you can replicate it successfully as a well-oiled business machine. You can afford to take more risk in this stage. For example, establish in-market experiments on where you can aim higher as a business. You will have the luxury of being able to dedicate some resources to think big—new products, new services, new geographies, and new partnerships. However, competition is probably also figuring out a way to grow or how to stall your growth, so some contingency planning is also required.

It is common in this stage for brand managers to invest in ideas that can be game changing for the category. These ideas could have up to a ten-year planning horizon. It takes time to deliver disruptive innovation. Skill-wise, leaders in this stage need strong operational discipline as well as an inspiring vision for future growth and potential.

Realignment (upward/downward)

Your business is doing well and your brand is stable. However, the business doesn't show an exciting progressive trend. This can happen because you and your team have been operating in the status quo for too long or you haven't noticed your external environment is changing rapidly and you are missing the waves. At times it takes a savvy competitor who is doing better than you to wake you up.

This phase requires deep understanding of what is holding the brand back, crafting a plan to remove those barriers and then generating a new sense of purpose to energize the organization. Brands at this stage are typically yearning for a breath of fresh air. A brand can be refreshed by looking at new customer groups to reach, identifying a future trend wave to ride or simply improve the existing product or service. From an organization perspective, realignment requires getting the full organization centered back onto a specific plan that will provide better results in market. The brand manager in this stage needs to over-communicate the brand's purpose, the new focus areas, and what no longer fits with the brand strategy. The organization needs to be very clear on what new strategy to execute against. In this phase, the leader also needs to seek strong buy-in and commitment from stakeholders to guarantee their support.

Turnaround (downward)

The brand has lost its true north. You have passed the threshold of acceptable periods of missing set business expectations of your stakeholders without major consequences. They are not happy with you. There is more of an upside than downside on making changes, so the brand manager is ready to take more drastic measures. Often there is a new team assigned to take charge of turning the business around from a downward spiral to an upward trend.

In this stage the brand manager needs to quickly demonstrate that a new strategy will give better results and again set the brand on a growth trajectory. It is common to completely rethink the positioning, the consumer target, and how the brand is executed overall. In this stage, the brand should only keep the few things that are working well and start to establish a new growth plan.

Divestiture (downward)

You have consistently missed expectations and the last two turnaround attempts have failed. Employee morale is low and you have already lost your best talent. The category is shrinking as your consumer base is growing old or has completely abandoned you for a competitor. The last equity health measure shows that your market value is less than half what it once was. In this stage, it is obvious the brand cannot sustain itself and comes to an end in the growth cycle. At this point there will be little to do from a brand-building perspective. The best thing to do is begin an exit strategy to either divest the brand or simply shut it down and let it disappear.

SUMMARY

In this chapter you learned how to assess the brand's environment using the internal and external assessment and capture it in a SWOT. You should be well versed now on what works and doesn't work for the brand and what it's strengths, weaknesses, opportunities, and threats are. The brand evolution cycles should have helped you determine where the brand stands on a spectrum of stages. Based on this you can forecast what type of growth strategy is best to pursue and how you will manage it through the brand-building journey. Having completed this set of analyses, you can put a stake in the ground on the brand's current state.

Now it's time to dream big! The next chapter will show you how to craft a vision and set goals for your brand in developing a brand strategy and marketing plan.

Vision & Goal Setting

"If you want to build a ship, don't herd people together to collect wood and don't assign them tasks and work, but rather teach them to long for the endless immensity of the sea."

—Antoine de Saint-Exupery

SETTING THE VISION

In the previous chapter, we learned where your brand stands right now. This chapter is about deciding where you want to go. This entails crafting an exciting vision and setting goals for your ultimate destination. Dream big! The vision is where you want to go, while goals are the steps that will take you there.

A bold, actionable vision will set your brand onto a trajectory for success. An excellent example of this is Howard Shultz's vision for Starbucks. Inspired by a trip to Italy in the early 1980s, he wanted to bring the Italian coffeehouse tradition back to the United States. Starbucks was to become a place for conversation and a sense of community—a "third place" between work and home. Shultz delivered on that vision. Today Starbucks has more than eighteen thousand stores in over sixty-two countries, delivering on their brand purpose to inspire and nurture the human spirit—one person, one cup, and one neighborhood at a time. By staying true to their original vision, Starbucks soared.[1]

There are many stories similar to Starbucks' of the positive impact bold vision statements can have on a brand. The best brand visions are the ones that are both rooted in reality, yet are audacious enough to hope for a better future. Acknowledging reality is recognizing a challenge. Being audacious is beating that challenge times two!

With a clear business challenge articulated and the current state well defined, you can begin to dream a little. Crafting a vision requires using all of the senses. The vision statement that captures where the brand is headed should paint a vivid picture of what that end state feels, smells, looks, and sounds like. It should be meaningful for everyone involved with the brand, employees, investors, and consumers alike.

Crafting the vision can be a very personal process for you the brand manager and one that requires careful thought. It requires sweat, maybe tears, and inspiration, as well as openhearted conversations with trusted advisors. There isn't a magical time frame that it takes to develop one—it can happen in a flash of inspiration or over a quarter of analysis, meetings, and discussions, maybe even longer. The goal is to craft a great vision that guides and inspires the organization to achieve its fullest potential.

Because of the personal nature of creating a "brand vision," instead of walking you step-by-step on how to craft one, I want to offer you two exercises that are helpful to get the process started. First, a framework to get your thoughts and ideas on paper and second, a set of questions to help refine the language of the actual vision statement that will travel across the organization.

> **"**If you want to build a great enterprise, you have to have the courage to dream great dreams. If you dream small dreams, you may succeed in building something small.
>
> For many people, that is enough. But if you want to achieve widespread impact and lasting value, be bold. **"**

~ **Howard Schultz,** CEO, Starbucks

Brand Vision Exercise

Putting thoughts to paper is not as easy as it sounds. Many of us become stuck when confronted with the infinite whiteness of an empty page. Where to begin? The journey begins, as they say, with the first step. Don't think too much; just start writing. Write without any kind of restrictions—no judging. The important thing is to get it on paper! Later we will go back to edit, refine, and tease out the amazing ideas that you didn't know were inside you.

To get you started, write down answers to these questions: Where is the brand right this minute? What does it feel like to be there with it? Does it make you happy? Proud? Sad? How would you describe it to a close confidant whom you were not trying to impress? Incorporate your work from the previous chapter into this description. What are its strengths and weaknesses? Try and make this description as vivid as possible.

Next, describe where you want the brand to be. What does success look like? Global recognition or perhaps something a little more modest? Dream big, but be reasonable. You can repeat this exercise every year as your brand and your vision of it grows. Again, try and be as descriptive as possible, not only of what the future looks like, but what it feels like. What meaning does it hold for its employees and customers? How important is it to their lives and why?

See, that wasn't so hard, was it? The next step is to read over what you've written and consolidate each description into a couple of concise statements. You might want to leave what you wrote for a while and come back to it with fresh eyes. Now, consolidate what you wrote into the following format.

First, the current status:
"Moving my brand from (insert the evolution stage from Chapter 3) with (insert strengths) and (insert weaknesses) . . .

Plus, the desired future status:
" . . .to being a brand that achieves (insert goal and/or purpose) and means and/or does (insert your strategy) for its customers/stakeholders."

This might all seem a little confusing at first, so let's take a look at an example to help you gain a better understanding of what you are trying to accomplish. Lego is a Star Brand recognized by generations of consumers that excels at establishing emotional connections with customers. Beginning as a small Danish carpenter's workshop, they have grown over the past eighty years to become the world's third largest toy manufacturer.[2]

What might their brand vision statement have looked like eighty years ago? It could have possibly looked like this: *"Move from being a simple woodworking studio to a toy manufacturer delighting children across Denmark."*

Of course, today, their vision statement might look something like this: *"Move from being the third largest global toy manufacturer to a brand that invents the future of play."*

This is all well and good, but it could be a bit meatier. Let's add a strategy and audience to make it more compelling. The more descriptive statement would read: *"Move from being the third largest global toy manufacturer to a brand that invents the future of play, by transforming the way that learning takes place to inspire and develop the builders of tomorrow."*

LEGO minifig, introduced in 1975

That statement is much more compelling, right? Great vision statements describe where you are moving from, where you are going to, and by what means you are going to get there. Let's look at the Lego statement again:

From: *"being the third largest global toy manufacturer . . ."*
To: *"a brand that invents the future of play . . ."*
By: *"transforming the way that learning takes place . . ."*
and finally, a compelling why: *"to inspire and develop the builders of tomorrow."*

Now, return to your vision statement. Does it have a from, to, by, and why? If so, great! If not, keep at it, it will come. Once you're happy with it, come back and let's make it better!

Vision Statement Critiquing

This exercise is intended to help you critique the vision statement that you are working on and make it better. A great vision statement is expressed in a simple but exciting way so others can connect with and champion it. It should capture the brand's uniqueness and strategic intent, as well as a bold stretching goal.

Run your vision statement through the following questions:

* Does the vision statement provide a powerful picture of what your brand will look like five to ten years from now?

* Does the vision articulate what your desired brand end-state will look, feel, and smell like? Use all your senses to describe it.

* Is the vision ambitious? Does it go beyond what is possible today? Does it represent a challenge worth going after?

* Does the vision encompass the sense of purpose for the brand?

* Does the vision language inspire and engage people? Is it memorable?

* Does the vision create a vivid image in people's head that provokes emotion and excitement?

Each of these questions should give you insights to refine the vision articulation to make it more powerful and meaningful. Once you have a great working vision statement share it with key stakeholders for input. You can also do the critiquing exercise above in a small group setting.

SETTING THE GOALS

Having completed the brand assessment and vision statement, then you are ready to set the brand goals. Without goals, your vision will never become a reality.

SMART Brand Goals are: Specific, Measurable, Actionable, Realistic, Timely

- **Specific:** It is clear what the outcome will be.
- **Measurable:** You can track progress and quantify success.
- **Actionable:** The steps to achieving them are concrete.
- **Realistic:** They can be achieved with the marketing strategy and plans you build.
- **Timely:** Resources and expectations can be set accordingly.

Every brand typically sets two goals: business performance and vision fulfillment. Quantifying progress of Business Performance goals is fairly straightforward. The most common metrics to determine a brand's business performance are: sales growth, market share, and profit growth. Measuring success towards a brand vision is much more subjective. It involves tracking things like brand equity, brand loyalty, brand awareness, etc., some of which can be more difficult to measure. In this chapter we will focus on the business goals and will cover intangible brand measurements later in the Measurement chapter.

Sales Growth
Sales increase is typically the main measure of brand growth.
It is based on the assumption:

Increased sales = increased customers = brand growth

Sales growth is expressed as a percentage of gross sales during a determined period vs. the same period of the previous year(s).

Common metrics of sales growth:
- Percentage of sales lift
- Index vs. prior year
- CAGR (compound annual growth rate) if you measure over longer periods of time

They all quantify the magnitude in which your sales improved vs. the period that is selected, commonly the previous quarter or year.

Sales growth expectations are linked to the financial expectations of the business in the short and long term. Sales growth expectation will be determined by the financial commitments the brand has based on its P&L. If the brand has been in market for some time, sales growth expectations could be linked to a multi-year growth plan. For newer brands with less reliable performance history, setting the sales growth target becomes more of a creative exercise taking into account any recent trends and best guesses on upcoming growth activities and market dynamics. The sales growth target could also simply be the sales needed to break even financially.

Market Share Position

In any product category, unless it is a monopoly, brands will be fighting for a stronger position in the market place they play in. A higher market position means more consumers are buying the brand and thus more sales are happening. Also, higher market position builds momentum for the brand's positioning in the marketplace, resulting in a stronger shelf presence, more brand awareness, etc. Therefore, market share is a key indicator of market competitiveness.

To survive in a highly competitive category, a brand needs to rise above a certain market share threshold to be a meaningful and sustainable player. Marketing plans can be built to deliver on specific market share position on a particular category, country, or region. However, it is really hard to forecast an exact number for market share considering that the performance of other brands in the marketplace is also a moving target.

The intent of this measure is to declare the position in the marketplace that you are going after, which can also be represented as the percentage increase of marketplace sales that the brand wants to own. The type of market share growth you expect will set the tone for the marketing strategy. Knowing the market share position you aspire to in this step will allow you to select the brand-building activities that will build competitive advantage, whether that is capturing a bigger chunk of the existing market sales or increasing category sales overall.

Profit

Star brands are profitable and should really be the goal of any brand. Brand growth should not come at the expense of profit, thus another core metric to use for goal setting is your brand's expected profit profile. This tends to be the most important metric when promising value creation to the key shareholders whom will evaluate the brand mainly as a business enterprise.

In simple terms, profit is what is left once you pay for all expenses, people, products, and employees. There are many different ways to capture profit measures and it can get very finance-heavy.

Common metrics of profit measurement:

- Percentage of profit growth
- Profit index versus previous year
- Gross margin
- Increase of percentage profit margin
- More complicated measures that capture value creation, which can be a combination of profit and cash flow metrics

The main intent of using profit as a metric to set your goals and later in the marketing plan is to ensure you are building your brand, growing sales and share while making profit. Profit goals could change year-to-year depending on the strategy the business decides to follow. For example, in light of major innovations or product launches the brand might choose to invest significantly more than previous years, which will affect profit. Also, if competition is really aggressive the brand can choose to defend its position by investing to close the gap versus competition in value, innovation, or appeal of offerings.

Sales, market share, and profit measurements intended to qualify the brand's growth profile are all interdependent. The more sales, typically the more market share and profit and vice versa. But we can only wish managing a brand was this straightforward. As a brand strives to increase sales and grow market share, it needs to spend more money, which will also impact profit, etc. So it is the combination of these three metrics that will determine the strategy for moving the brand toward your overall vision.

BRAND STRATEGIES

The goals become the anchor to select the brand strategy. With clear brand goals, you can craft a brand strategy and plan to deliver on it. Recall the brand can be in any evolution stage at a particular point in time. In order to move forward from that stage, the brand will need to follow an intentional brand strategy. Business development theory explores four core strategies that brands can pursue to accomplish their goals: Growth; Sustain; Defend/Protect; Harvest. The selection of one of these brand strategies will depend on how well the brand is doing in market given its strengths and weaknesses, as well as consideration of overall market dynamics.

The brand goals precede the strategy. Each strategy will have a different combination of sales, market share, and profit goals. The goals that you set to support the vision will influence the brand marketing strategy that you develop.

Below are the objectives and characteristics of each strategy that you can pursue and their relationship with the goal metrics: As you read through them, refer to the chart at right that summarizes how the three core metrics could vary by strategy and main characteristics. You can use this chart to set the goals for your specific brand based on your current state and your future vision.

Grow	Sustain	Profend	Harvest
Objective			
Fuel momentum to maintain competitive edge	Maintain advantage vs. competition	Protect sales and market share at the expense of profit	Achieve profit with little market share growth
Assessment			
Significant strengths and opportunities	Sustained strengths and strong market position	Threatened by a competitor's advantage	Weak overall but still breaks even financially
Potential			
Growing category	Mature category	Risk of commoditization or emerging price competitor	Declining category or brand appeal
Sales			
⬆	⬆ / ➡	➡	➡ / ⬇
Greater than prior year	Greater or equal to prior year	Equal to prior year	Equal to or less than prior year
Share			
⬆	⬆ / ➡	➡ / ⬇	➡ / ⬇
Greater than prior year	Greater or equal to prior year	Equal to or less than prior year	Equal to or less than prior year
Profit			
⬆ / ➡	⬆ / ➡	➡ / ⬇	➡
Greater or equal to prior year	Greater or equal to prior year	Equal to, or less than prior year	Equal to prior year

Growth Strategy

Brand builders are rewarded for growing brands and the positive sales impact that result from it. Following a growth strategy requires a brand's sales and profit to be significantly higher than the previous year or previous performance cycle.

A growth strategy is not only what meets the financial expectations of the key stakeholders in the company, but also what ensures that a brand has a sustainable business model so it can continue to be available in the market. This strategy can be expensive and is important to have funds available like working capital and resources such as marketing and research and development to unleash further growth.

To grow a brand, a marketing strategy and plan need to demonstrate that it will yield higher sales than a year ago, improve the brands market share position and ideally maintain—if not improve—the overall profit structure of the brand. To grow the brand significantly versus the previous year, brands can use a combination of marketing tactics. Some brands will launch new products, ideally disruptive innovation that challenges the existing category norms. Brands will request more marketing investment versus previous year, re-prioritize investment choices, or get more efficient. In the case of a growing category, brands that are looking to grow disproportionately will also want to expand into more consumer segments as well. From a competitive standpoint, a growth strategy requires that the brand proposition have a competitive edge versus competition either in consumer appeal, market advantages in pricing, or distribution. The marketing plan in a growth strategy setting will need to prioritize funds accordingly to continue to fuel this competitive edge.

Sustain Strategy

A sustain strategy equals steady growth. In this strategy, sales, share, and profit expectations will remain equal to or higher than the previous year. Maintaining these metrics, however, implies growth. The market dynamics are not static so this strategy assumes that the brand sustains its appeal in market and strong market fundamentals, which also require sustained investment.

Compared to the growth strategy, a sustaining strategy implies more measured and consistent growth; likely more applicable to a mature category and/or years when the brand doesn't have any major product innovation or funds available to grow expansively. The marketing strategy for sustained growth is likely to include product launches like line extensions of existing products versus major innovations that require significant dollars to drive awareness among consumers. The marketing plans for a sustaining strategy will require similar levels of investment as the previous year. From a competitive advantage point of view, this strategy calls for sustained support of the previously successful core marketing mix fundamentals which can include pricing, retail partnerships, key marketing vehicles, etc.

Protect and Defend

A protect and defend strategy is used when market dynamics have changed and are threatening the brand's ability to deliver sustained sales, share, profit, and long-term growth. This is a common strategy when a competitor has a major innovation launch that is driving disproportionate share growth or aggressively lowering prices to win market share. When a brand is in this situation, growth expectations need to be revisited. Even delivering at the same performance level versus the previous year could become an unrealistic goal.

In light of aggressive competition and the need to defend the brand, it might be okay to sacrifice some short-term profits to protect the market position and retain any competitive advantage the brand has enjoyed up to this point. This strategy requires a careful balance of short and long-term investment choices in order to defend the most valuable turf of the brand. Marketing plans for this strategy will likely include fast product changes such as claim or packaging changes. Another common tactic used to protect market share is changing the pricing and promotion strategies to match an aggressive competitive brand. However, this can be a risky game to play as it could turn into a price war where all manufacturers lose in the long term due to price depression. A successful protect and defend strategy is one that limits the long-term impact of the competitive activity and sets the brand to resume a sustain or growth strategy.

Harvesting

The strategy of harvesting is used when you have a business that doesn't have long-term potential or the brand has lost significant competitive advantage, yet still delivers positive cash flow and profit. The intent is to harvest the benefits of the brand's current status without investing significant resources. This strategy is also commonly referred to as a "milking" strategy.

In this situation, the brand sales and profit should be positive, but it is expected that the market share of the brand will fall back due to lack of investment or potential. Eventually, a harvesting strategy will result in a divestiture or shut down of the brand. The lack of investment in the brand will result in a self-fulfilling prophecy of brand value erosion over time. If the strategy is to "milk" the brand, there shouldn't be any new product introductions or significant marketing spending. The financial strategy is such that keeping the brand alive represents a cash flow advantage and profit that can be reinvested somewhere else. In the case of a portfolio, if the brand appeal has significantly tampered or lost significant differentiation or competitive edge in the market place versus other brands, the harvesting strategy can be used to redirect any funding to other brands in the portfolio with more potential.

SUMMARY

By successfully completing Step 1: Brand Assessment and Goal Setting on the Star Brand Model, you have established an anchor point and a destination for your brand-building journey.

The brand's current state—defined by the internal and market analysis—gives you the "you are here" arrow on your brand's map. The vision and goals that you set have shaped the type of marketing strategy that you will develop in the upcoming chapters. Figuring out how the different components of your brand strategy and marketing investment choices will drive the sales can help you develop the building blocks needed to deliver on your goal.

A robust brand assessment and an inspiring vision will serve as a solid credential and foundation to the brand's marketing strategy and brand growth plan to be developed. As you continue to move along the five steps of the Star Brand Model, think about how you can move the brand from its current status to the ideal business destination as determined by the vision and goals. Each step will give you new information on the set of choices the brand can make to reach its ultimate potential, thus creating step-by-step a brand building strategy. Completing the five steps will result in a brand-building strategy to take the brand from its current status to the desired star status.

You are now ready to move to Step 2 in the Star Brand Model, Defining Brand Equity and Target, which is the journey to define what your brand will stand for in the hearts and minds of consumers, and which of them you want to really delight.

An inspiring vision will serve as a solid credential and foundation for the brand's growth.

LEGO wooden toy duck,
circa 1935

Questions & Review

Questions to assess your brand and market:

- What business is the brand in? What does the brand sell and make money on?
- In what markets/territories does the brand compete?
- In what categories does the brand compete? Who are its competitors?
- What is working for the brand?
- What is not working for the brand?
- What environment forces are influencing the brand? Financial and brand equity health, consumer trends, technology, category-specific trends.
- What are the brand's top five strengths?
- What are the brand's top five weaknesses?
- What are the brand's top three opportunities?
- What are the brand's top three threats?
- What development stage is the business on? Describe recent successes, failures, and most significant brand milestones to date.

Questions to set goals and a vision:

- What does stardom status mean for your brand—how does it feel, smell and look?
- What is the brand's vision?
- What are the goals behind the brand's vision? How does that translate to sales, market share, and profit?
- What is the best brand strategy to pursue based on the brand's evolution stage, SWOT and growth expectations?

Defining Brand Equity & Target

5

Defining
Brand Equity

"If this business were split up, I would give you the land and bricks and mortar, and I would take the brands and trademarks and I would fare better than you."

— John Stewart (Former CEO of Quaker)

Brands have an intrinsic value in the market place; they are assets of the business they belong to. The value of brands is based on the theory that a well-known brand is likely to generate more sales than one that is lesser known, as consumers will perceive the products or services of a well-known brand as superior. Therefore, a brand creates equity, or value, by having a recognized brand name that is associated with a particular product or service offering. The stronger the brand's value, the more sales the brand is likely to generate in the marketplace and vice versa.

A brand's equity is made up of all the elements that make it distinctive, including its products, communications, and visual expressions. Brands with better products, more effective communication, and highly recognizable visual expressions will create more brand equity. The job of a brand manager is to build the equity of the brand they manage by manipulating all the core marketing elements to be more effective at attracting more consumers to the brand.

Thinking about a brand's equity is akin to thinking about what a brand will stand for to create value. Consider this Step 2 of the Star Brand Model, the brand's introspection chapter. The "Know Thyself" mantra applied to brand building. Recall one of the key reasons Star Brands are successful is because they possess great clarity. They know what they offer, why they offer it and how to offer it in a unique way. A great deal of effort was put into defining their brand equity. It was intentional, as brand equity drives creative decisions, visual identity decisions, as well as business decisions. So any brand that wants to succeed should strive to do the same—have a clear articulation of who they are, what they stand for, and then communicate that effectively. The goal of this chapter is to help you achieve that for your brand.

Creating and nurturing your brand's equity is an ongoing creative process and it should be well documented to drive clarity of execution across the broader organization. Brands typically create a "Brand Bible," which documents core components of the equity, as well as containing operational guidelines. This document is used solely for internal purposes and is rarely shown to the public. It contains the "secret formula" of your brand, so to speak—the components with which you create brand equity in the market. It's not the advertisements, packaging, or product designs of the brand; rather, it contains the ingredients used to create those assets.

Brand managers will often carry the brand equity document with them as their playbook. It will have multiple uses to inform agencies they work with, help write creative briefs, influence future innovation projects, and serve as a decision guide in management meetings.

Brand equity can be a bit of a fuzzy topic, so let's make it a bit more concrete by diagramming it. In 1998, Kevin Lane Keller, a marketing professor at the Tuck School of Business, developed a model that organized the core elements of a brand into the shape of a pyramid.[1] Each component worked as a building block

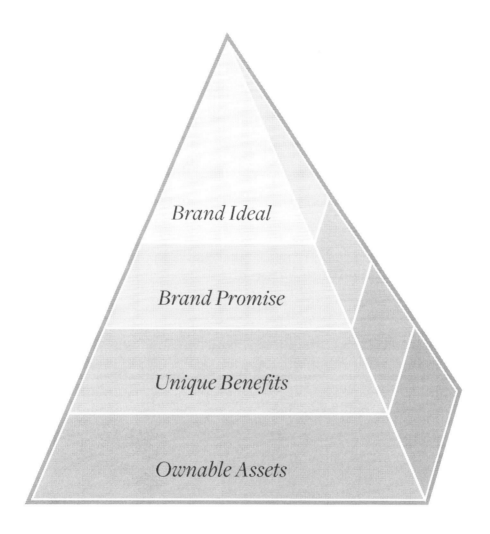

Brand Equity Pyramid

The core components of the Brand Equity Pyramid are rooted in many of the same characteristics of Star Brands; higher order purpose, emotional connection, and superior benefits.

to shape how consumers think and feel about a brand. Their strength would create more or less brand value. This is still the most common visual representation of the brand equity concept. The pyramid device is effective because it represents all the components of a brand and gives them order. It results in having the different components to build on each other in a supporting role. I will use a pyramid to visualize the brand equity concept as well.

The core components of the brand equity pyramid are rooted in many of the same characteristics of Star Brands; higher order purpose, emotional connection, and superior benefits. The core components of the brand equity pyramid are:

* Brand ideal
* Brand promise
* Unique benefits (that set the brand apart)
* Ownable assets

In the pyramid structure, the core brand equity components are organized in ascending order. At the bottom you have the consistent assets that people will visually recognize, in the middle you have the emotional or functional benefits that your brand offers, and in the top you articulate the way in which your brand uniquely delivers these benefits and assets. All of the pyramid's building blocks ladder up to an inspiring ideal, the brand's reason for being, its "why."

BRAND IDEAL

Brand ideal is the reason why the brand exists and why it creates the products and services it offers. Everything the brand does should ladder up to this. In some companies brand ideal is also referred to as mission or brand purpose. The ideal is the brand's "why," the reason the brand is in business. Oftentimes the ideal comes from the original inspiration for the brand, its early beginning or the reason why its first product was built. The ideal is the special something that attracts people, stakeholders, and employees to be part of it.

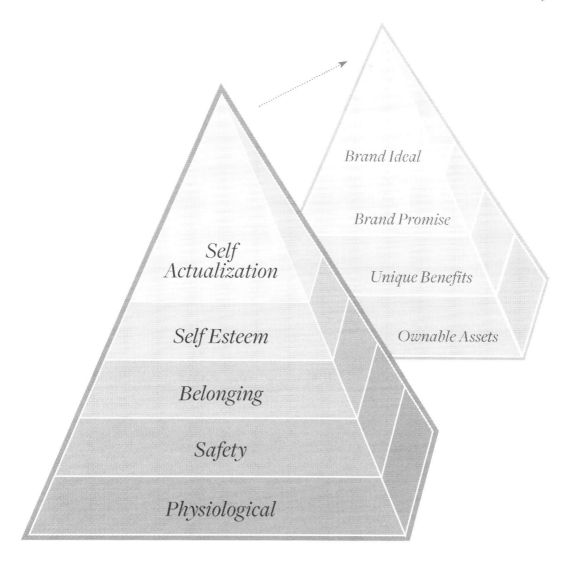

Maslow's Pyramid

The Brand Equity Pyramid was inspired by Maslow's "Hierarchy of Needs", with Brand Ideal and Self Actualization as similar goals.

Capturing a brand ideal in a simple sentence is a great way to ensure continued focus on that ideal as the brand grows. Every decision can be held up to it as a litmus test.

A brand ideal is articulated by completing the following statement:

"We exist to _____." or

"We believe in _____."

This statement needs to be meaningful and make a difference in the life of the consumer. The best brand ideals speak to the consumer's need of self-actualization, which is the peak of Maslow's famous Hierarchy of Needs, a human's desire for self-fulfillment and reaching full potential.[2] Brand ideals can, at times, feel lofty and highly idealistic, but that is ok as long as it is distinctive and truly supports the brand's soul and "why." The articulation of the brand's ideal needs to work for your brand, your employees, and your target consumer once you execute against it.

To learn more about the ideals behind Star Brands, I met with Jim Stengel, former Global Marketing officer of P&G, who today is dedicated to helping brands grow based on their ideal[3]. A few years ago, Jim had the hypothesis that brands with a higher ideal experienced higher rates of success. Upon his retirement from P&G, he wanted to quantify this concept and make a living helping brands achieve success via their ideal. In partnership with the research firm Millward Brown, he conducted a study of fifty brands that quantified the value of leading a business based on ideals. The study showed that these fifty ideal-led companies had generated a return on investment 400 percent better than the Standard & Poor's 500! Proof that a well-defined brand ideal is well worth developing and nurturing. The detailed findings of his research are presented in his book *Grow: How Ideals Power Growth and Profit at the World's Greatest Companies.*

Beyond market results, which are indeed impressive, Jim spoke of feeling a special energy at the ideal-led companies he visited. After every visit, he left feeling like he could stay and work there. The cultures of these companies were magnetic—they emitted positive energy. These companies expressed why they were in business and communicated it across their entire business operations. It was not just one person's idea or a marketing plan for the short term. They were ideal-led from top to bottom. Here are some examples:

Discovery Communications, which includes the Discovery channel, has achieved extraordinary results behind the ideal of "curiosity." This ideal is embedded in the company's values and it is measured in employees' performance reviews. They host inspirational offsite meetings for employees all designed to nurture the value of curiosity.

IBM was once one of the greatest companies in the world, but they lost sight of their ideal. They have since recovered by focusing on the ideal of being "essential to the world." They have three values and nine practices that allow IBM to remain focused as a global organization. IBM's management is confident that if the practices are executed, they will succeed. They are now living their ideal inside and out. If you look at their advertising campaign "Smarter Planet" you will see that it is a clear expression of the company's "Be essential to the world" ideal.

Method, premium household cleaning products, is so committed to championing healthy cleaning in the home that they redesigned their manufacturing process to be more environmentally sustainable and community friendly. They built a new plant and distribution center in the south side of Chicago that will offer a park-like area for the local neighborhood. The plant will have a power-generating wind turbine mill that you will be able to see from the highway. Quite iconic.

Uber, the tech startup and car service app, is a great example of a company committed to an ideal with no compromises. Uber's ideal can be broadened to be "helping people have things immediately delivered to them." They are also reinventing transportation. You can see that their ideal is much more encompassing than the current car services they offer. The company is gaining momentum delivering against this broader vision.

Having a compelling ideal is a secret of successful Star Brands. It works as a guidepost that allows a brand to go beyond the product offering and really put a stake in the ground on the higher order benefit that the brand gives to the world, which in turn will help establish longer lasting relationships with like-minded consumers.

To find an ideal for your brand, or to improve upon one you already have, start by looking at fundamental human values. These values will orient your search.

The "Smarter Planet" campaign is a clear expression of IBM's "Be essential to the world" ideal.

Method redesigned their manufacturing process to be more environmentally sustainable and community friendly.

Ask yourself these questions about the brand you are building:

* Is the brand helping achieve status or other types of self-actualization? (here are some of the higher order needs humans seek: exploration, creativity, morality, achievement, spontaneity, respect, confidence, bonding, legacy, acceptance, and solutions)

* What type of positive emotions does the brand create?

* Does the brand help establish connections? How does the brand impact the society positively?

* What would the brand or company founder(s) say inspired them to create the product? What human need(s) were they moved to satisfy?

Answering these questions will help you craft your brand's ideal. If you are stuck, looking at other inspiring ideals can help as well. Here are some of my favorites from my conversation with Jim and inferred by looking at brands. They do a great job of being aspirational, distinct, and wide-reaching.

Organize the world's information and make it universally accessible - *Google*

Empower creative exploration and self-expression - *Apple*

Empower people to positively impact food culture - *Chipotle*

Celebrate journeys of progress and success - *Johnnie Walker*

Celebrate timeless luxury craftsmanship - *Hermés*

Democratize fashion trends - *Zara*

Energize the world - *Red Bull*

Make the world of commerce simpler, more flexible - *MasterCard*

Deliver happiness through WOW service - *Zappos*

Fulfill dreams of personal freedom - *Harley Davidson*

BRAND PROMISE

If brand ideal is the reason for a brand to exist, the brand promise is how the brand delivers on that ideal. The brand promise is a statement of what the brand uniquely offers to capture the hearts and minds of its consumers. You can think of it as the ultimate core benefit the brand offers to solve a consumer need.

A brand's promise sets expectations for consumers in terms of benefits and experiences associated with its products and/or services. It sets the tone for the type of brand interactions the consumer should expect. Exposing current and prospective customers to the brand's assets that communicate that expectation, such as marketing communication and visual identity, will reinforce that association over time.

The brand needs to deliver on its promise in every brand interaction. It should be a positive experience for the consumer. The consumer expects the brand to deliver on its promise every time, hence the importance of consistency when building brands, a core characteristic of Star Brands.

Brand promise articulations are considered the brand's positioning strategy and typically only used internally within the organization and not with consumers. It is the basis for brand communication briefs, research and development inspiration, and input for internal meetings. It also serves as a guidepost and filter to determine what marketing executions and product or services ideas are "brand right" and which are not. Thus, the brand promise also becomes a stewardship tool in the brand-building process.

In some instances, the brand promise statement can be used externally as well. If the brand promise is well-crafted and descriptive, it can be used with consumers, for example, executed in the form of a brand tagline—a short message accompanying a brand's logo. However, these are hard to come by as taglines and brand promise statements serve two different purposes and audiences. For example, you might recall these famous taglines:

Got Milk? - *California Milk Processor Board*

Just Do It - *Nike*

Think Different - *Apple*

Think Small - *Volkswagen (Beetle)*

I probably didn't even need to mention the brands associated with these taglines because they are likely already in your mind. These taglines are brilliant, but probably not descriptive enough to work well as a brand promise statement. Let's look at these brand promise articulations instead: [5, 6]

The ultimate driving machine - *BMW*

The short-haul, no frills, and low-price airline - *Southwest Airlines*

Magical Fun Family Entertainment - *Disney*

Authentic Athletic Performance - *Nike*

The hardware department store for do-it-yourselfers - *Home Depot*

A strong articulation of the brand's promise typically delivers on the following characteristics:

* Drives differentiation versus competition and generates consumer preference for the brand. Encompasses the benefits that set the brand apart and its core visual identity.

* Relevant to your target. Ultimately, this is the group of consumers you should be most interested in persuading with the executions of your brand promise.

* Written so tightly as to be memorable—strive for less than five words.

* Links to the category the brand plays in. This specificity makes it more available and actionable for the organization. It also crafts a space for the brand to carve it's own niche in the marketplace.

* Language is inspirational and leaves room for growth so it motivates the organization to execute against the brand promise consistently.

UNIQUE BENEFITS

A brand's role is to solve consumers' needs with the unique benefit it offers. The functional and emotional benefit a brand offers is what will set it apart from competition. These benefits should answer the target consumer's deepest needs across the spectrum of physiological to self-fulfillment needs. Ideally brands should have both functional and emotional benefits to speak to both the heart and mind of their customer. Functional benefits can be related to performance, aesthetics, or tangible attributes that the consumer experiences using the product. Emotional benefits can be related to social benefits, feelings that the product activates, or higher order benefits such the need for validation and self-actualization.

Michelin's iconic "Bibendum" represents the brand's functional as well as emotional benefits.

Marketing theory commonly talks about brand benefits as points of difference and points of parity. There will be benefits that you will be very good at and therefore strive to own in the market place. Those are called points of difference. Points of parity are benefits you also offer as a brand, but your performance and the way that you offer them will not be superior versus competition. Some equity pyramids will list them both. Now, why waste the time talking and worrying about characteristics that everyone else has? With the intent of being selective in your brand equity pyramid, I recommend you only focus on the benefits that can be truly differentiating, ownable, relevant to your target, and will set you apart in the marketplace. The intent is to continue to invest in these benefits being truly superior versus any other product or service offering. You typically can only execute three or four that your brand excels at anyway. Since you won't be able to communicate more than three to four messages effectively in market (unless you have very large marketing budgets) be selective and focus on the brand's main points of difference.

The brand points of difference that you select for the equity pyramid will be used in multiple places and brand-building tasks: advertising briefs, informing innovation programs, choosing where to expand features, to name a few.

Once the benefits that set you apart are in your brand equity pyramid, the brand needs to stay committed to using and communicating these choices to consumers consistently.

Here are some examples of benefits that a brand might choose to put on their equity pyramid if they set the brand apart from competition:

Functional

* Performance—e.g., Detergent brand: Best stain removal; Deodorant brand: Odor protection that lasts all day
* Aesthetics Features—e.g.,. Orange juice brand: Environmentally friendly packaging; Technology brand: Sleek, simple design
* Usage—e.g., Software brand: Intuitively simple, easy to use
* Ingredients—e.g., Skincare brand: Patented rejuvenating formula

Emotional

* Relationships—e.g., Pet food brand: Helping you keep your dog healthy and thriving
* Self actualization—e.g., Counseling Services: Helping you connect with your best self
* Personalization—e.g., Entertainment brand: Customization of music that unleashes your expression
* Status/ Validation—e.g., Leather goods brand: 100 years of craftsmanship heritage; Luxury clothing brand: Designed and curated by an Italian designer

The unique benefits that set you apart are reasons for the consumer to believe in your product. These choices live at the core of the brand and should not change over time. You can find new ways to talk about them to keep your communication relevant and fresh, but the benefit itself should be the same unless the needs of the consumer you serve dramatically change.

OWNABLE AND RECOGNIZABLE BRAND ASSETS

If equity is the value of your brand, your ownable and recognizable brand assets are the currency of your brand. These assets are typically housed within the brand's visual identity and physical manifestations. These branding choices represent your brand and you wouldn't want any other brand to use them. You own them; they might even be copyrighted. These ownable and recognizable assets are the triggers that will help a consumer recognize the brand when exposed to it. To fully own an asset, it must be distinctive and undeniably linked to your brand via consistent use over time in the marketplace. These assets will work as unifying glue that your consumers will uniquely associate with your brand.

The Starbucks logo is a valuable brand asset recognized around the world.

Since the brand assets are long-term bets, they need to be brought to life in market executions with excellence. The quality of the brand's execution is really what the consumer experiences. It is the responsibility of the brand manager to protect these valuable brand assets. Any changes to them should be carefully considered, as they will likely have an impact in market and ultimately on sales.

A brand's packaging is perhaps its most important asset. The more time I spend with designers, the more I realize the immense power packaging has on communicating the message of your product and a marketing idea. Design matters. The 3D shape, the 2D graphics, communication and ease of navigation, and all critical components of your packaging can set your brand apart. When your package is done right, there is no need for a lot of words. There isn't need to supplement the package with more communication on shelf. Amazing packaging tells your brand or product's story immediately—what you stand for, your superiority, and the number one emotion you want to trigger. Brilliant packaging design triggers a visceral reaction that makes it simply irresistible to buy. Your eyes and heart buy the packaging. It should be love at first sight. So work to get it right. Packaging can become an ownable and recognizable asset for the brand.

Some brands follow an intentional process to develop assets. Brand managers will work with either design managers in their teams or design agencies to fully define the brand's visual strategy and iconic assets. The definition of these assets typically goes hand-in-hand with defining the brand equity and communication. After defining the assets, the brand manager and design team can determine how to best manage these assets across communications to achieve the desired consistency.

Once the brand's visual identity and ownable assets are developed, they are reflected in a brand book or brand visual identity guidelines. This type of document becomes a proprietary tool and is used to educate everybody who needs to touch the brand to create marketing executions such as people in the organization, agencies, or executional vendors. This management process of the brand's ownable assets ensures the assets are properly manipulated when handed off to third parties.

Finally, even if you have a lot of great assets that define your visual identity, they won't all go into your equity pyramid. Only the iconic assets that are truly indispensable for your brand to be recognized should be listed. Also, there should be assets that have a strong market value tied to the brand's unique positioning.

Here are some examples of types of assets that well-recognized brands could list on their equity pyramid given the level of recognition and association they have established with the brand.

- Logo: Starbucks, Nike
- Sound: Intel, Harley
- Shape: Coke, Beetle
- Color: Tiffany
- Pattern: Burberry, Louis Vuitton
- Photography Style: Abercrombie and Fitch, Ralph Lauren
- Typography: Disney
- Smell: Westin "White Tea scent," Cinnabon
- Icon: Marlboro Man, Pillsbury Doughboy, Michelin Man

HARLEY DAVIDSON EQUITY PYRAMID

Now that we've reviewed the components of a brand equity pyramid, let's take a look at a fantastic example of one, which truly becomes greater than the sum of its parts—Harley Davidson, an undeniable Star Brand. I have never ridden a Harley, but as a brand builder I deeply admire what this brand has accomplished, and I will refer to it several times throughout the book.

This American motorcycle manufacturer sold its first bikes during the first decade of the twentieth century. With determination it moved successfully across brand evolution stages. It survived the great depression, a period of poor quality control and strong competition from Japanese manufacturers, and tackled a relevancy problem with attractive new consumer targets. With over one hundred years in business, today Harley is considered an iconic brand. It has created such devotion and loyalty that "Harlistas" and devoted Harley riders freely and happily tattoo the brand logo on their bodies. The brand has found success creating strong communities of Harley enthusiasts all over the world, becoming in turn a solid global brand with over $5 billion in sales still rooted in a strong American heritage.[6] Based on reading multiple papers, case studies, and studying many market executions of Harley, here is my interpretation of how a Harley brand equity pyramid would look.

Brand Ideal—The reason Harley does what it does:
Harley exists to fulfill dreams of personal freedom.

Harley proudly displays this statement as their purpose on their website. This ideal is powerful because it speaks to the brand's target need of self-actualization. Dreams are inspirational. Personal freedom celebrates the uniqueness of the individual. Freedom is a core value of the Harley Davidson brand.

The Brand Promise—How Harley delivers on this ideal:
Harley offers an Authentic American Motorcycle Experience

Brand Ideal
Fulfill Dreams of Personal Freedom

Brand Promise
Authentic American Motorcycle Experience

Unique Benefits
V-Twin Engine, Craftsmanship, & Heritage

Ownable Assets
Logo, Engine Sound, Bike Design, HOGs

The Harley Equity Pyramid

After more than 100 years in business, Harley has built an incredibly strong Brand equity supported by every level of the equity pyramid

Authentic encompasses the unique benefits appealing to the core target. American speaks about the attitude of western freedom unleashed in the ride. The word motorcycle establishes a connection to the specific industry in which the brand plays. The promise of each brand will be different and there isn't an exact formula. In the case of Harley, this statement articulates what the brand offers to the target, the emotions associated with it, and declares the industry space in which the brand will play.

Unique Benefits

Most products can claim multiple benefits. If you list all of them, it may begin to feel like a laundry list. Selecting a brand's core points of difference is a strategic choice. Strategy requires sacrifice and determination. With the intent of picking three to four core benefits for Harley's equity pyramid, I considered the most distinctive benefits that would speak about the functional and emotional benefits of the brand. I selected a combination of benefits that spoke about the product performance itself, a higher order benefit, and its heritage. They all ladder up to the brand promise and brand ideal.

Powerful ride with V-Twin engine technology

Perhaps the most famous performance feature of Harley Davidson motorcycles is the engine. The V-Twin engine innovation premiered in 1908 when Walter Davidson rode a Harley Davidson to victory in a race.[6] That was the first of many races and the beginning of the brand's journey into stardom. Over time, Harley has continued to invest in improving and innovating this technology that delivers the power of Harley motorcycles. This ongoing investment in the engine is a sign that it is a benefit that sets it apart from competition. This point of difference speaks to the performance characteristics of the bike and qualifies the experience of riding it as powerful.

Craftsmanship that enables customization

Craftsmanship speaks to attention to detail and unique design. Customization adds authenticity to the Harley experience. Since Harley is about individuality and freedom, customization is a benefit that supports the brand's promise. This benefit holds well to Harley's multiple customization options for the bikes such as colors, engines, leather finishes, accessories, etc. Harley invites customers to build their own Harley as a way to set themselves apart from other riders.

110-year Heritage

Harley prides itself on a long-standing reputation as a motorcycle manufacturer. Their heritage adds substance. It also builds credibility for the first time buyer who may be unsure of the brand's history. The 110-year heritage can also be qualified as "110-year American heritage." However, in the case of this specific benefit I chose to leave the country qualifier out to make it more flexible for global expansion considerations. At times, associations with a specific national-ity can limit the relevance of your brand when expanding outside the original territory.

Ownable Assets

Harley has done a masterful job of defining its visual identity. It's a designer's dream in terms of consistency of visuals and strength of emotion portrayed. The brand is so distinctive and iconic that I selected four main ownable assets. These

The latest evolution of Harley's motorcycles honors their 110 year heritage with a v-twin engine and powerful profile.

are the elements of the brand that (in my opinion) have the highest marketplace value given their high level of recognition by consumers, distinctiveness, and association with the brand.

HD Logo:

Widely recognizable icon and logo. It has a shield and a bar that makes it bold and powerful. The colors are the Harley orange, its own Pantone color, and black. It is consistently used across geographies and in marketing executions over time. It is also placed on Harley merchandising, which drives recognition around the world even by those who don't own a Harley.

Motorcycle shape, low profile motorcycle:

Speaks to the unique characteristic of the Harley look. The heavy and low profile layout and position in which people ride them sets them apart from other motorcycles.

Sound:

Harley Davidson motorcycles have a very distinctive sound/roar. The sound is intentional and only possible with the Harley Davidson design. Most Harley television commercials will feature the sound of the bike.

Harley Owners Group (HOGs):

In general, marketing execution choices, celebrities, or public relationship assets are not ownable assets—they are executed in the short term and change over time. However, in the case of Harley, the Harley Davidson Owners Group—HOG—can be deemed an ownable and recognizable asset. The main reason is that HOGs have now become indisputably distinctive and recognizable—some consumers get a Harley just to be a HOG. The HOGs have been a proven marketing strategy since 1983 and continue to be a very visible and recognizable brand expression.

You can see from this Harley equity pyramid how carefully chosen each building block in the pyramid needs to be and also how all of them ladder up to the brand's ideal. All the equity pyramid components are critical elements of the brand's positioning in the marketplace. The equity pyramid becomes a stake in the ground as to how the brand intends to create value and is a way to begin crafting the brand's marketing strategy, inclusive of the brand's communication choices.

SUMMARY

Thus far in Step 2 of the Star Brand Model, you learned how a brand needs to become crystal clear on what it will stand for in the hearts and minds of consumers and how it will create equity in the marketplace. This process entailed defining the brand ideal, promise, and a set of benefits and ownable assets that support the brand pyramid and drive differentiation. Upon this introspective brand exercise, we are now ready to define in the next chapter the target group of consumers to whom this equity pyramid will be most relevant.

6

Selecting a
Brand Target

"An archer cannot hit the bullseye if he doesn't know where the target is."

— Anonymous

We can't be everything to everybody. It is exhausting and almost impossible to do. The same is true for brands. Your brand won't appeal to all consumers in the marketplace. It can also get very expensive to try to reach everybody. Thus, you shouldn't try to cater and talk to all consumers. You should define and select the unique type of customer that you want to attract and delight. Having a unique target in mind will help focus your brand's efforts, such as communication and product development, where they matter most.

Defining and selecting the type of customer you want to target for your brand is a critical decision in brand strategy. Your target becomes a choice of where you allocate your marketing and research and development resources. Selecting a distinct consumer target to pursue will drive focus on your innovation efforts, your marketing efforts, and ultimately will be the source of your short and long-term business growth. Having a target will help you prioritize those efforts and allocate resources where they will give you the biggest return. Understanding your target will also give a clear roadmap of what you need to do to improve your brand experience to maintain their loyalty.

One of the most important tasks of a brand manager is to identify the right target group to pursue. This stage in the brand-building process requires thorough analysis and strategy determination. The effectiveness of your marketing efforts will depend largely on how well defined and actionable the target is that you select. You also need to determine if you need a few well defined targets versus only one to accomplish your long-term goals. Once you find the right target you, as the brand manager, should become intimate with this group of consumers – understand their needs, what makes them thrive, their life insights, and ultimately the role your product can play in their lives.

Amitava Chattopadhyay, the GlaxoSmithKline Chaired Professor in Corporate Innovation at INSEAD, and author of *The New Emerging Market Multinationals: Four Strategies for Disrupting Markets and Building Brands*, shared a powerful yet simple targeting example with me from one of the companies he studied.[1]

Mahindra & Mahindra is an emerging Indian automobile company. One of its hero products is its tractors. They are small, reliable, rugged, and fuel-efficient.[2] Mahindra tractors were very successful in India, so the Mahindra management team was looking to go outside the country to find the next big market.

The most obvious way to look for a new, international target would be to identify locations that had consumers with similar demographics—gender, age, ethnicity, income, etc. Segmenting consumers based on demographic is a common practice, but one that offers very limited insight into whom these consumers really are or what they want.

The Mahindra team was aware of the bias that a demographic segmentation posed. They knew that finding new expansion targets for their tractors via demographics wouldn't give them the insight they needed. This approach would have limited results, likely ending with a marketing plan to sell Mahindra tractors to Bangladesh or Africa, which were arguably not attractive markets. Instead they asked themselves the question, Which other consumers around the world are looking for similar benefits of what the Indian consumers are demanding? This questioning allowed Mahindra to segment their target based on needs versus demographics. Mahindra was looking for potential targets that had similar needs to the Indian customers they were serving at home and the Indian customer target was looking for small, reliable, and efficient tractors

At the time, the management team used secondary sources and their own expertise to conduct a needs-based segment analysis. As some Mahindra managers had been educated in the United States, a lucrative potential market, they decided to investigate whether or not there was a corollary needs-based segment in the United States similar to the one in India. Much to their surprise, they found an exact match! As it turns out, hobby farmers and landscaping firms in the United States have exactly the same need for small, reliable, and efficient tractors as Indian farmers. More importantly, their needs were currently not being met by any product in that category. What a discovery!

"Which other consumers around the world are looking for benefits similar to what the Indian consumers are demanding?"

Upon identifying the matching needs segment group to pursue in the United States, the management team decided to begin exporting Mahindra tractors. This was the best way to prove if the needs based target match theory would work. The Mahindra team found a dealer in the Southern United States willing to carry their tractors and they began selling them. It was a match —the brand took off because of the strong fit between the product and the target consumer they identified. The product was so successful that Mahindra quickly expanded in the United States and began building its own manufacturing site.

Today Mahindra has three plants in the United States and continue to do very well as a provider of small, reliable, and efficient tractors. Once they got their targeting strategy right and they knew that it was working, the next logical step was to find other countries with a high incidence of their needs segment. They moved to Australia next, a logical step to reach an additional significant number of hobby farmers with the same product. Expanding globally with a common product line-up across markets is still yielding significant dividends to the company. Mahindra now focuses on delighting consumers around the world that have a great passion and love for the land they work with and want to get the job done in the most efficient way possible.[3] Needs based segmentation was a core strategy in Mahindra's international expansion approach and certainly increased their rate of success.

Mahindra's tractors success story demonstrates the power of identifying the right target for your brand. These three consumer groups, Indian original target, American hobby farmers, and American small landscaping firms—all with obvious demographic and attitude differences—belong to the same need segment: light to medium tractor activity. A small, reliable, and affordable tractor like Mahindra's meets that need perfectly.

Focusing on their current Indian's buyer demographic characteristics (and not the need) would have likely triggered a very different brand strategy and arguably change the course of the expansion plans. This example highlights the importance of asking the question which consumers are looking for these benefits to meet their needs. Once they understood the needs segment they served very well, it was possible for them to find similar segments to serve and expand their global footprint with the same product. Mahindra tractors didn't follow the classic segmentation process or sophisticated market research tool. They used second-ary data along with their own market understanding and first went in small to mitigate risk before expanding. This approach worked because they focused on needs to segment and select their target market. That is the power of needs–based segmentation.

In this chapter you will learn how to identify a target for your brand much like Mahindra. I will walk you through a series of steps to define, refine, and investigate the best target for your brand.

There are four steps in the targeting process:

* Segment your market
* Select your target needs segments
* Select your target sub-segments (if needed)
* Meet your target

Let's explore each step in depth.

SEGMENT YOUR MARKET

Segmenting is a way of organizing your universe of customers into meaningful and distinct groups. There are many different ways to define these segments—demographics, attitudes, behaviors, values, or needs. Most importantly these segments or groups should be distinct, stable, and specific to your category.

There is a natural temptation to segment your market according to demographic data. In my experience this results in many indistinct groups that tend to change over time. Psychographic data, such as values and behaviors, similarly falls short in articulating the customer relationship to your product. Only a needs-based segmentation strategy, as demonstrated by Mahindra, can truly, and distinctly, capture common drivers of consumer choice.

Needs are what consumers would describe as the main reason they enter the category of products or services you offer. By focusing on the needs of your target consumer, your brand can meet them with the benefits your product or service offers. You can then build a range of product or service offerings that will serve the distinctive needs in the market. Focusing on needs first, as it is the primary reason why consumers choose the product, is a more reliable way to select consumer segments.

After identifying a needs-based segment, you can dig deeper and explore the lifestyles, behaviors, and demographics of your target. Rather than starting with these variables to define your target, you are using them to help refine and better understand a specific needs based category, which in turn will help you better communicate with that audience.

Today consumers exhibit a range of needs from the purely physiological, at the bottom of Maslow's pyramid, all the way up to self-actualization. The explosion of brand choices we see in the market today is the result of companies willing and eager to cater to these needs in every conceivable category.

Consider the recent explosion of bottled water in the American market. Currently, in the United States alone, there are more than seven hundred brands of bottled water. Seven hundred. The product doesn't get any simpler. It is H2O. The range of bottled water brands available is simply mind-boggling. How can a market support so many brands—brands whose product you can essentially get for free right out of the tap in your kitchen? The answer is needs based segmentation.

The proliferation of bottled water in the US over the last decade owes more to segmentation than to thirst.

Let's break down some common bottled water
brands into Maslow's categories:

* Status - *Acqua di Cristallo Tributo a Moldiglian*

* Lifestyle (Aspiration) - *Sparkling Perrier*

* Health Conscious/Natural - *Evian*

* Finest in Retail - *Fiji Water*

* Personalization - *Flavored Water*

* Refreshment Accessibility - *Dasani*

* Physiological Need - *Tap Water*

The basic need of hydration can be solved by any of them, however each brand is trying to satisfy other needs in the pyramid: from the locally bottled brand for less than $2; to more common Dasani, Evian, and Fiji that have broad global distribution; to more aspirational options like the luxury Acqua di Cristallo Tributo a Moldigliani, which sells at $60,000 for a unique gold-coated bottle gathered from "the world's best springs."

With competition as stiff as it is in the bottled water market, big companies would study the market carefully to determine in which segment they should compete in. They would typically hire a research firm to conduct a complete quantitative needs based segmentation using surveys of large samples of actual consumers. Which, depending on the size of your brand, is certainly an option. Once the surveys are completed and the data processed, the researcher will use statistical models to combine variables to arrive at an ideal number of distinct groupings of consumers that share similar characteristics and similar drivers of choice. Then the brand manager could begin to select brand targets from these quantitatively defined need segments groupings.

Now that you understand the benefits of using needs based segmentation to segment your market, let's dive in and create one! To start the segmentation process, map out all of the various needs customers in your particular category might have. Maslow's Hierarchy of Needs, just as you saw in the water example, can be a great tool to help you create needs segments. Using each needs category in his pyramid, create a list of needs for your particular product category. Don't just list needs fulfilled by your brand currently, list needs fulfilled by the category or sector in which your brand competes. Each section of the pyramid can help you organize main distinct drivers of choice, or reasons why consumers select your brand. Then organize the list into the most meaningful buckets of needs. The output should be distinct needs segments for your particular category that you can then choose a target(s) to delight with your product(s) or service(s). Let's look at an example:

I've created a hypothetical blue jeans brand in order to show how you can define the target for your brand even if you don't have resources to conduct deep market research. All you need is knowledge of your market and a few simple tools.

Let's call our new blue jeans brand "Classé Denim." Its brand ideal is to make denim luxurious. Its brand promise is to be "The Haute Couture of Denim." The product is hand crafted in Italy and designed by a group of fashion and body aesthetics experts. The brand's current marketing mix focuses on driving awareness and appeal of the brand via print advertisement in high-end magazines alongside a strong public relations campaign targeting influencers and celebrities in the thirty-five-plus age range. Distribution-wise, Classé Denim jeans are only sold at high-end department stores like Saks and selected online retailers. Its jeans are priced 5 times higher (5X premium) than regular Levi's jeans or similar brands

To select our target consumers we need to first segment the blue jeans market. This includes all possible consumers that might be interested in buying a pair of jeans, not just Classé jeans. The first questions to ask are: Why do people buy jeans? What are the different needs people have that a pair of jeans could fulfill? We can answer these questions using Maslow's Hierarchy of Needs.

Some consumers will buy jeans simply because they need a basic pair of pants as a clothing option (physiological). Heavy duty or construction workers that wear jeans for work will be looking for sturdy jeans and their primary driver of choice would be durability (safety). Other consumers would buy jeans that make them look good or even hide their imperfections (self-esteem). Others will insist on finding the right type of jeans brand that can signal they are part of a unique group and want to be admired (belonging and status). These distinct needs-based groups—there could be many others—will segment consumers by common-

Brand Ideal
Make denim luxurious

Brand Promise
Haute couture of denim

Unique Benefits
Luxury Fit, Body Experts, Crafted in Italy

Ownable Assets
Logo (assuming it's widely recognized)

Classé Denim Equity Pyramid

alities on lifestyle and attitudes or shopping behaviors, but the most important driver that defines them should be the reason why they need a pair of jeans.

We now have a basic structure of needs for the blue jeans category. We identified four segments worth investigating further: basic jeans, durable jeans (intended for work), jeans that improve figure, and status jeans. This structure is the foundation for selecting a needs-based segment(s) for Classé Denim. We will continue to build on this example as we go through the additional segmentation steps.

SELECT YOUR TARGET NEEDS SEGMENTS

With your needs segments categorized, it is time to select targets whose needs your brand can best fulfill. As a brand manager your task is to find the most valuable consumer segment (or segments depending on the size of your brand and your long-term growth goals) upon which to focus your efforts.

Many consumers will buy your products, but the majority of the sales will typically come from a smaller, but very valuable set of customers. Many brands still experience the 80/20 rule: 20 percent of their core customers are responsible for 80 percent of their business. You need to identify who your core customers are today and who will be the core customer in the future.

A brand can play across multiple segments if it is big enough and has a broadly appealing positioning. A multi-segment target works for a brand as long as the overall brand positioning is relevant to all the segments and the range of product offering is wide enough, or can be tailored, to cover the needs of each unique group.

So, if categories can be segmented by different needs, how do you know which one is right for your brand? There are two criteria to help you make your choice: Equity Fit and Attractiveness.

Equity Fit

The role of a brand is to solve consumer needs and establish a relationship with the consumer in a way that is relevant and resonates with him or her. The way the brand solves the consumer needs is by bringing to life the benefits and core elements that were identified in the equity pyramid. These benefits are only relevant to the needs segment that cares about them. Therefore, your choice of equity will also determine the appropriate needs segment to go after.

Unless you want to change your brand positioning—which you may consider if you're changing your growth strategy—you should only target segments to which your equity is relevant. Answer these questions for each of your segmentation groups. If the answer is yes to all of them, continue to keep them in your list.

NEEDS-BASED SEGMENTATION

Define Segments based on Maslow's Hierarchy of Needs

Physiological

Buy jeans for simple
clothing options

Safety

Buy jeans for utility
and durability

Belonging

Buy jeans to belong
to a status group

Self-esteem

Buy jeans to
feel good about
appearance

Answer these questions for each of your segmentation groups

- Is your brand equity statement relevant and appealing to this segment?
- Does your brand have a unique way to deliver the benefits that will solve the main need of this segment?
- Do your brand benefits rank high in importance for the product category you compete in if you were to ask your target consumer? (You can actually conduct some research to answer this.)

If the brand promise is not relevant, that is probably not the right target to go after. If the benefit a potential target consumer cares most about isn't an attribute at which your brand excels, then you shouldn't spend your efforts there. Play in areas where you can offer superior benefits to delight your target consumer in areas they really care about.

Attractiveness

The segment you go after should be worth your efforts and resources. There will be needs segments that are valid, but not big enough to pursue. Segments can prove unattractive either because of their actual size (it is only a small percentage of the population) or they promise limited growth potential.

Here are a few questions to ask:

* Is this needs segment large enough or have enough growth potential to give you the sales growth you are expecting?

* Do you think the product that you will offer can be profitable based on what the consumer in this segment is willing to pay?

Answering these two questions can roughly confirm if the segment or segments are appropriate for your goals. Calculate how many consumers from your needs segment you will need to attract to meet your goal. This can be done by making some assumptions on the number of expected sales per consumer and how many you think you can effectively reach. If the segment is sizable enough to meet your sales growth expectations, move ahead and go deep to understand this segment. If your brand charges a premium price, understand how price sensitive the consumers in each segment are and roughly how many of them would really consider buying your brand.

By applying the equity and attractiveness filters to select the right segments, our Classé Denim jeans brand target model would look like this:

Equity Fit:

* Our brand's benefit of luxury custom fit appeals to two segments that we discovered: the self-esteem group looking for jeans that improves body figure and the belonging group looking for a brand that boasts status

* Our brand can distinctively deliver on both of these consumer needs. This positioning would not appeal to the basic jeans group or the durable, safety group. Therefore, we would discard that group based on equity fit.

NEEDS-BASED SEGMENTATION

Define Segments based on Maslow's Hierarchy of Needs

Physiological	*Safety*	*Belonging*	*Self-esteem*
Buy jeans for simple clothing options	Buy jeans for utility and durability	Buy jeans to belong to a status group	Buy jeans to feel good about appearance

Filter segments by Equity Fit and Attractiveness

Physiological	*Safety*	*Belonging*	*Self-esteem*
Buy jeans for simple clothing options	Buy jeans for utility and durability	Buy jeans to belong to a status group	Buy jeans to feel good about appearance

Attractiveness:

- Classé Denim needs a 25 percent sales increase in the next year.
- Current sales are 20,000 units per year, so our new needs segment(s) needs to deliver at least five thousand new customers each year.
- As a luxury brand, Classé Denim needs to look at the price sensitivity and possible income levels for each segment in order to determine the receptivity to premium pricing.

We determined that only consumers in the "status" segments and the "improve figure" segment are likely to pay a significant premium for their jeans. And within each segment only one third of consumers are likely to pay as much as five times premium pricing. Based on the finding, to deliver on the brand's five thousand sales goal, we might need to select both segments as a starting point and go deeper to understand each better and decide if we can market to both. The good news is that the range of the Classé Denim product line-up will be able to satisfy the needs of both segments well.

SELECT YOUR TARGET SUB-SEGMENTS

The third step in brand targeting is to determine whether you need a sub-segment strategy to further unlock growth in the short term. Once you have the model that segments the different needs in the category and select your core segments, you might still wonder if, by focusing your efforts even further, you could increase the reach of your brand.

If you are in this situation, dig deeper within each segment and see if there are meaningful differences or other defining characteristics that are not being met with the current market segmentation.[4] If the answer is no, you are done. You can focus on delighting your current needs segments. If the answer is yes, you will likely benefit from identifying what type of sub-segments within a core segment could be addressed with more precise marketing strategies to further serve customer needs and unleash more sales potential. The sub-segment can then become

NEEDS-BASED SEGMENTATION

Define Segments based on Maslow's Hierarchy of Needs

Physiological

Buy jeans for simple
clothing options

Safety

Buy jeans for utility
and durability

Belonging

Buy jeans to belong
to a status group

Self-esteem

Buy jeans to
feel good about
appearance

Filter segments by Equity Fit and Attractiveness

Physiological

Buy jeans for simple
clothing options

Safety

Buy jeans for utility
and durability

Belonging

Buy jeans to belong
to a status group

Self-esteem

Buy jeans to
feel good about
appearance

Identify Sub-segments

Create sub-segments if unique
differences can be identified
in order to increase short term
marketing performance

the brand's prime prospect for growth on a specific marketing initiative. However, you should only identify a sub-segment if you are planning to act on it.

Sub-segments can push you to focus your marketing efforts further and accelerate brand growth. For example, they can dial up the effectiveness of tactical short-term marketing objectives like product or sub-variants launches, seasonal messaging, etc. You can easily choose a different sub-segment the following year if your marketing tactics or product offerings get updated. The addition of sub-segments can also open customization opportunities that can allow a business to add additional value and strengthen the relationship with potential customers. The key however, is that your sub-segments still stem from your main needs segment and core target for the brand.

Sub-segments can be built based on behaviors, attitudes, life stages, or any differentiating characteristic that creates a sizable enough cluster of consumers worth targeting. Looking at behaviors, for example, you can consider consumers that are entering the category for the first time. If you are a feminine protection brand, you can create sub-segments of girls that are going through puberty and need to buy feminine protection products for the first time. If you are an insurance company, first time home buyers or first time car buyers could be a great sub-segment to target marketing efforts on a particular year or to accelerate brand trial.

Depending on the strength of your brand, loyal or heavy users of your product could also be a strong sub-segment for unique marketing efforts. Focusing on loyal users could be a great sub-segment strategy if you are repositioning your brand and want to reduce the risk of losing them. On their own, these groups of consumers might not be a long-term need segment on their own, but they could make a great sub-segment to one of your core needs segments.

Another common sub-segment strategy is based on relevant demographics. For example, in the United States several brands are following an ethnic sub-segment strategy by targeting Hispanic, Asian, or African American consumers within a particular product or service category. Ethnic consumers in the US are growing at a faster rate than non-ethnic counterparts. In some categories, ethnic consumers exhibit significantly higher spending and potential growth than other groups. Thus, an ethnic group with significant growth potential for your category, used as an additional differentiating characteristic as part of a need segment, can be a quite powerful sub-segment to focus on to accelerate growth. You can easily activate marketing strategies like promotions, specific advertising, and different language activation among the ethnic target while still staying true to the need segment to which they belong.

Multicultural marketing has become a key accelerator of growth for many brands. However, if you decide to have an ethnic sub-segment, you need to invest in really understanding this group of consumers and creating communication that really speaks to them versus simply translating your advertising language or changing the ethnicities of the cast in your commercials. If you want to grow with ethnic consumers, go to school on multicultural marketing and get it right. There are several strategy firms and multicultural advertising agencies that can help with your multicultural strategy.

In the case of Denim Classé jeans brand, while we selected two robust needs segments to target and investigate further, perhaps there is benefit to identifying sub-segments to focus marketing efforts on. If the brand's most important initiative next year is to promote their classic style line up, perhaps talking to Boomer generational cohort, women born between 1944 and 1964, can make marketing efforts more effective. Boomers are also more likely to have disposable income and afford more luxury items. Having a "classic-cut lover boomer" sub-segment as part of your need segments might give the brand additional focus for that year's marketing efforts. Another example of a potential sub-segment for Denim Classé could be "high income new moms" that want to look good again in jeans. They are most likely wearing a new size and have the need for a custom fit jean. This can be a sub-segment to focus on in the short term for the segment of consumers looking for a jean to improve their figure. Finally, given the luxury positioning of the brand, Classé Denim could also choose to make its sub-segment "luxury seekers" that fall under its selected needs segments. This can add further focus to all its marketing efforts.

As you can see from these examples, the type of sub-segments a brand chooses will depend on whether there is a benefit in going deeper within existing selected segments to capitalize further on specific marketing programs.

MEET YOUR TARGET

Congratulations! You now know how to identify and select which need segments you want to focus on, as well as a potential short-term sub-segment if needed. The final step is to meet your target and make it come to life.

To get to know your target, first identify a few core characteristics or questions derived from the needs segment you selected. If you did a quantitative segmentation you will likely get an algorithm (core questions and answers that allow you to assign consumers to your need segment). If you defined the segment yourself, you can create drivers questions like what is the main reason you are interested in this product/service.? If you already have a hypothesis of some distinctive characteristics, e.g., age, activity, lifestyle, you can use those in addition to the category drivers.

Once you have defined your target consumer based on needs segments, equity fit, and attractiveness, get creative on how to find and deeply understand them. You should really try to meet them in person and talk to them. The goal is to put yourself in the shoes of your consumers. The best insights come from observing them and connecting the dots between secondary data and real life consumer verbatim. The best consumer research is that which allows you to understand who the consumer is as a full person—aspirations, habits, and surroundings—ideally visit them in their real environment versus a focus group facility. At times with consumer research, the real answers are in what you see versus what the consumer tells you. Many brand choices and purchases are sub-conscious, thus it can be hard to easily articulate why we buy what we buy. We often use default answers that we think might be accepted. However, there are clear patterns that indicate why we make brand choices. These patterns are more tangible than we think; you can spot them with good observation techniques. Our homes, how we dress, how we spend our time, the transportation method we choose all show our drivers of choice as a consumer. Given that there is more than meets the eye when talking to consumers to gain insights, marketers need to have a more journalistic and inquisitive approach when they talk to them.

Nine Ways to meet and understand your target:

1. If you have a store where you sell food or other kinds of products, come up with incentives like free product or random drawings for your customer to spend some time talking to you. This is your chance to ask a range of questions in person to better understand them—from what they think of the product to who they are as a person.

2. Build a panel of consumers you can talk to regularly that fit your target. Get to know them well. Invite the same group to pizza or coffee. The group dynamic can help you discover more about them as well. If you can use a research supplier, schedule in-home visits or join one of their friendly get-togethers.

3. Try to come close to the environment where your target consumer lives. If you are interested in household chores or food, make sure you schedule the visit during those times he or she is thinking of or preparing to use your product. Pay attention to non-verbal cues of what surrounds him or her.

4. Use the product as your consumer would. Even if you are a man managing a brand for women, use it. Actually going through the experience with your product or the category just like your target would is a great way to get in touch with the needs and tensions of the consumer.

5. If your brand is active in social media like Facebook and Twitter and there are consumers that you think fall on your target that are "friends" with you, contact them and ask for permission to interview them.

6. If you know how much your target spends in a typical week, try to live on that budget for a week yourself. This exercise puts you in your consumer's reality and lets you experience why he or she is making certain brand choices.

7. If your target happens to be older, try to simulate the experience of shopping for your products as if you were older. Try wearing dark glasses and gloves to adjust your senses to what your target sees. If you have a target that is likely to bring her or his kids along to shop with them, try simulating this experience as well. You might realize how little attention will be available to select your brand.

8. If your product is a service, go through the process of signing up for the service from beginning to end. I am always surprised how many marketers in the service industry haven't gone through the process of signing up for the service they market.

9. Have you ever considered examining the purses of your target consumer (with their permission of course!)? You will be amazed how much a woman's purse and its contents tell you about what is important to her and what tools and products she decides to carry along with her. The type of purse she chooses can also give you real hints as to the type of activities she attends and how she manages her time during the day. We tried it for a project in class to better understand a consumer target for a particular brand and it was really eye-opening!

Once you have a good understanding of your target, you can get creative bringing it to life. Create a visual representation of the consumer in his or her full expression—the whole persona. Begin documenting the key characteristics and traits of your target. Use visuals and clear examples to illustrate what drives your target, their preferences. You can even make a full life-size cardboard printout of your target so you and others are reminded of it everyday. The more tangible the image of the target consumer you are going after, the better. Use all of your senses to describe and bring them to life.

Make your brand target real by giving it a name. If your target is composed by different needs segments, create distinct personas for each group. Also, make the consumer profile simple so it can be memorable at all levels of the organization—those employees closer and further from the consumer. Use it consistently. Repetition will make the target consumer definition memorable and each individual in your organization will feel personal ownership of it.

To make it easier to identify a target for you and others, use a set of core questions that defines your need segment. It can be a fun team activity for each member to find out which segment they fall into. This will help further internalize the concept of your target.

Here is an example of the type of info that you should collect:

SAMPLE PERSONA CHART

"Inspirational quote that reflects the target's beliefs and personality"

Target Bucket i.e., "Aspirational Shopper"
Short bio summing up the target's relevance for the brand.

Demographics	Traits & Values	Media Consumption	Brand Habits
30 Year old woman	What she believes in	Websites	Preferences
College Graduate	What makes her happy	Movies	Trial Barriers
$75,000 salary	Anxieties	TV Shows	Use Patterns
2 kids	Ambitious	Magazines	Shopping Habits
Married	Educated	Books	
Owns car		Music	

Once you have a tangible consumer profile, you can use this tool to educate your organization and most trusted partners, including creative agencies. A brand's target is typically included in advertising briefs and internal marketing planning meetings, and used by other departments such as Research and Development to inspire product innovation. A brand's target is a useful tool to influence the direction of many strategy conversations and processes.

Finally, the better your team knows the target the more they will be able to use it to inspire their work. Now that you know your target, invest the time to introduce it well to your organization. If you do this well, your organization will rally around the target consumer and use it as a guide on their daily work. That is targeting strategy in action.

To wrap up this chapter, I want to share a great example on how to share your consumer target understanding in a unique way. Paul Smith, storytelling coach and author of the bestselling book *Lead with a Story,*[5] shared it with me.[6]

Paul was working as a consumer researcher at a major consumer goods manufacturer conducting a big segmentation project. He and the sales team wanted to share their segmentation learning as a selling point at a meeting with the retailer client, one of the major retailers in the United States. Thus far the team had not been successful in getting the retailer's support to promote its brands and growth strategy. So the meeting needed to be a big sale.

For the meeting, instead of using PowerPoint, the team decided to follow a more unusual approach to persuade the retailer. The meeting began with the team leader pulling out a chair for a special guest he introduced as the "Achiever Mom." The audience found this really awkward, but went on with introductions. Soon enough the anticipated guest arrived. The audience immediately recognized this special guest. She was one of the Marketing Directors from the manufacturer, but for today she was introduced as the "Achiever Mom." The executive was, in fact, an "Achiever Mom" by the segmentation algorithm the manufacturer used to define its target segments. She had answered the set of questions from the segmentation and fit this segment perfectly. She met all the qualifications to represent this consumer at this meeting with the knowledge from the research team and her own personal experience. There was an awkward silence. Then the executive from the manufacturer leading the meeting asked the audience, "What would you like to ask her? She is your 'Achiever Mom.'" The questions started to come slowly at first. But as the audience realized the Marketing Director they knew was indeed also an "Achiever Mom," questions like "How often do you shop at our stores? What do you buy there? Where else do you shop? Why don't you buy that stuff at our store?" continued rapidly. She answered all the questions from the audience authentically. The audience went on and on inquiring enthusiastically. Question by question they were getting a more vivid image of what this target segment was all about—what she liked, where she shopped, why she bought certain products and her aspirations—all perfectly embodied in the manufacturer's Marketing Director they knew.

By the end of the meeting, the retailer team was convinced about the value of going after this target. After all, they had met the "Achiever Mom" in person that day. It was real and relevant for them. They asked the questions they cared most about. The risk the team took paid off. They turned an abstract definition like a segmentation and needs segment into something concrete for their client. The retailer was so bullish after the presentation that it reorganized its entire management structure around the target segments presented that day. Paul raves about this being the most serious organizational commitment to a customer segmentation strategy he has ever seen a retailer make.

This exercise of making the target consumer more tangible for a partner and using a specific bold delivery tactic paid great benefits for everybody involved— the manufacturer, the retailer, and ultimately the consumer they serve. That is the power of bringing your target consumer to life to influence business choices.

SUMMARY

Now you have learned the great benefits that come from identifying a brand target to focus all your marketing efforts. We explored how needs-based segmentation will help you segment the market and select the right consumer to disproportionately delight with your brand. I demonstrated that you could conduct this exercise fairly easily even if you don't have a lot of resources to complete a full market study. The magic will come in really selecting the right consumer group to focus on, understanding them deeply, and then acting on the learning.

It is the quality of your consumer target understanding that will make your marketing and communication efforts more effective. That is what we will learn next in Step 3 of the Star Brand Model, Crafting a Communication Strategy. With a brand equity defined and a consumer target selected in Step 2, the next step is to dig into insights, benefits, and ideas to communicate your brand positioning effectively to your target. We are well on our way to building a robust marketing strategy for the brand.

Questions & Review

Questions to help define brand equity:

* What is your brand's ideal? Why does it exist and make the products or service it offers?

* What is your brand's promise? What does it stand for?

* What are the brand's benefits and strengths? How does it compare to competition?

* How would you define the brand's voice?

* What are the brand's ownable assets? Are they recognizable?

* Do all of the brand-building blocks ladder up to the brand's ideal at the top of the equity pyramid?

* How consistently are your visual identity choices and ownable assets executed across consumer touch points? Use a scale from one to ten.

Questions to help define and select your brand target:

* Who is your current brand customer? How has this customer evolved?

* How do you segment your customers? Which needs can your category be segmented by?

* Is your brand target large enough to deliver the business goals?

* Is your brand relevant to all the customers you talk to?

* What type of sub-segments do you have? Do you need any sub-segments?

* How does your brand identify and connect with the target consumer?

Crafting a Communication Strategy

7

Insights,
Benefits & Ideas

"Creativity is not a talent, it is a way of operating."
— John Cleese, on what drives creativity

John Cleese, the English comedian and co-founder of the Monty Python, gave a lecture in 1991 on the five factors that drive creativity. It is brilliant, and filled with his signature cultural insights and wit. He talked about creativity not being a talent available to just a selected few, but a way of operating that allows you to generate ideas. Instead of a talent per se, creativity seems to be the ability to operate between two thinking modes. One thinking mode is "open," to diverge and ponder; the other one "closed," to converge and implement a specific solution with precision. The most creative people are those who play longer with ideas and set aside the discomfort of wanting to resolve them right away. "Be in the open mode longer," he says.[1]

As a marketer, I found this concept of creativity both enlightening and empowering. Many people get into the marketing profession because they want to create. The closest thing to actually creating in the business world is advertising. Advertising can then be considered an art with a consumer-desired response in mind. It is often a brand manager's most exciting job duty.

Ads are to marketers what candy is to kids. Marketers actually don't mind watching commercials. While most Americans look forward to Superbowl Sunday, marketers look forward to the day after. This is when you can watch all the ads without interruptions, read the reviews, and evaluate the work on your own. This includes discussing them with others and dissecting them to understand why they work or why they don't. It's a day of complete inspiration! Whether you consider yourself a creative person or not, you can learn how to operate in a way that fosters creativity. And you will need to be creative to deliver in this step of the framework in order to come up with insights and benefits that will become ideas and advertising executions to build your brand.

In Step 3 of the Star Brand Model, we will identify what message will resonate most with your core audience to drive purchase decisions and build brand loyalty. By this point, you should have completed the previous two steps. Your brand equity, promise, and benefits can now be transformed into an effective advertising message, aimed at the brand target you identified in the last chapter.

The core elements of any brand communication are insights, benefits, and ideas, which I will refer to as IBI. Insights and benefits are inputs in the advertising brief, the document that a client uses to contract an advertising idea and executions with creative agencies. After the brief is created and submitted to the agency, the agency responds with an idea, which is the creative transformation of the insights and benefits that you briefed. The idea is what is then turned into advertising executions that will reach the consumer across media touch points. I will explain each of these concepts in more detail and give you examples of how these ideas become advertising. In this chapter, you will also learn how to build an advertising brief which you can use for your brand if you work with an advertising agency. The ultimate objective is that you learn in this step how to build a communication strategy for a brand, which is a creative development process

Before we get started with all the theory, let's pause for a moment and reflect

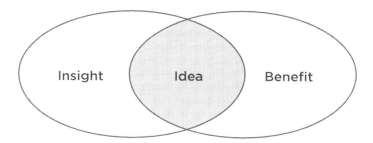

on what makes IBI so effective and powerful. The reason advertising works, the reason consumers have brand loyalty, is because of deep-seated human emotion. We all have hopes, desires, and fears. The interplay of these emotions with the reality of the world around us creates tensions within us that need release. Brands can have a powerful effect on the inner life of human beings and it should be treated with the utmost respect and care. A brand shouldn't create artificial needs or tensions. Instead, one should strive to truly understand and sympathize with a consumer's emotions in order to effectively connect with them. I really believe that the best brands truly touch consumers' lives and make them better by solving some of their needs. Please keep this in mind as you manage your brand. We are now ready for IBI. The first I is . . .

INSIGHT

What is an insight? An insight is an accurate and deep intuitive understanding of a human truth. In the case of a brand, a consumer insight is a discovery of an inconspicuous human truth, often combining bits of knowledge, and actionable via a tension that touches the consumer's heart and is worth resolving.

To sell a brand promise in your advertising, you first need to offer a strong hook that grabs the consumer's attention. Insights are the hooks for a brand to establish a connection with the consumer. Without a relevant hook, the consumer might not be open to engaging with your message. Having a hook in communication is the key to the consumer's heart and mind and it typically comes in the form of an insight that is weaved into the advertising.

Insights can come from anywhere but the best insights come from interacting directly with your customer, by talking and listening to them. It can also come from simple observation or the analysis of trends or quantitative data. At times, it will take a combination of first-hand data and secondary information to craft the right insight.

Ideally the insight should come from your target consumer for it to connect deeply with him or her. This is the best way to bring your target consumer into the advertising development process. If you get the insight right, the consumer will know that you really understand them. Then your advertising will be more effective.

While there isn't a formula per se to generate strong insights, there are a couple of characteristics to look for when you are developing them. First, they need to be true and almost universal. Second, they need to be discovered—it is not yet obvious, and requires a deeper understanding to identify them. Third, it needs to be emotional and logical at the same time, so it stems from a deep feeling or behavior the consumer exhibits. Finally, there should be a need or a tension that hasn't been resolved. If there is no tension in the insight, there won't be a role for the brand and advertised product to play.

A great insight articulation is one that includes a tension that you can't resist to solve with your brand and bring to life in advertising. The insight is the trigger for the brand to connect to the consumer and serve its benefits.

Here is example from the beauty category of a universal insight giving birth to a brilliant idea for an existing campaign. Dove, the personal care brand, discovered through proprietary research that women were missing out on capturing some of life's most memorable moments because they were anxious and not happy about the way they looked. According to the Dove global research, 77 percent of women are camera shy, citing that they often feel self-conscious or uncomfortable having their photo taken because they do not feel beautiful.[2] Building off this insight, Dove built the "Camera Shy" idea, an extension of their existing "Real Beauty" campaign. The ad juxtaposes grown women who hide from the camera versus young girls who adore camera attention. The spot ends with the

□ flawed?
□ flawless?

Is beautiful skin only ever spotless? Join the beauty debate.

campaignforrealbeauty.co.uk 🕊 | *Dove*

Dove's original research on women's relationship to beauty led to the insights behind the "Real Beauty" campaign.

bold question, "When did you stop thinking you were beautiful?"—raising the question of why women hide from the camera as an adult, but loved the camera as little girls. This tagline masterfully captures the insight and connects with the heart and mind of the consumer. This is a great example how quantitative data and deep understanding of the consumer led to the discovery of a breakthrough insight which in turn became great advertising.

Dove Camera Shy Analysis

* **Insight:** When you are little, you play up to the camera. As a woman you hide from the camera because you stopped thinking you are beautiful.

* **Tension:** I want to be as confident as I was as a girl.

* **Campaign Idea:** Camera Shy. When did you stop thinking you were beautiful?

The insight that soccer fans are a form of family led to a 41% increase in organ donation.

Another great insight example comes from soccer. Activating a strong insight in advertising has the power to change behavior for the good of society. This is what one of the winners at 2013 Cannes International Festival of Creativity—think the Oscars of Advertising—did by creating the first ever organ donor card for a soccer team, Brazilian Sport Club Recife. The campaign "Immortal Fans" developed by Ogilvy Brazil encouraged soccer fans to become immortal fans by registering as donors.

The public health campaign was fueled by a great insight and tension. Access to transplant organs is a grave health challenge in Brazil. Organ donation is limited due to families not wanting to give authorization because they don't know where the organs are going. Understanding this barrier, the agency looked for a consumer group where this tension could be solved. And they found a great one. They identified a group of committed fans from a specific soccer team that wished they could be part of their team forever. The solution: organ donation as a great way to do that. They could donate to those that would guarantee to continue to root for their beloved team.

To bring the idea to life, the agency recruited real patients on actual transplant waiting lists to send the message to the fans directly. "I promise your heart will always beat for Sport Club Recife," was the message to the fans from a woman awaiting a heart transplant.

The fans of Sport Club Recife wanted to be fans forever and now they can. Over fifty-one thousand people registered for a donation card and organ donation in Brazil has increased by 41 percent.[3]

Sport Club Recife Analysis

* **Life Insight:** From passionate fan: "My team is my life, my family."
* **Tension:** I wish I could be part of my team forever.
* **Campaign Idea:** Immortal Fan.

The idea of Immortal Fan gave Brazilians a reason to donate organs and discuss with their family their wish once they received their donor card. An impressive life-changing result from this insight–led campaign.

Both insights in the Camera Shy and Immortal Fan examples are true and almost universal. They could apply to many consumers around the world. They both required a deeper understanding of the consumer to arrive at the insight, which at first was not obvious. They are emotional because they deal with deep human desires and logic because there is tangible compensating behavior from the consumer to cope with, like hiding from the camera or refusing to donate because you don't know where the organs are going. These brilliant insights were properly executed in advertising and married with a clever presentation of the benefit to solve the consumer's need, generating a very positive transformation in consumer behavior.

Crafting a strong insight for an advertising brief is more an art than a science. It's hard to identify insights and requires a few attempts to arrive at a clever articulation. It requires a lot of careful listening and finding just the right language to capture the essence of the insight. You need a crisp articulation of the insight to make it actionable. When you have a great one, you just know it. If someone hears it, it should get a big "wow" expression and ideally the person feels that the insight they heard is a truth that applies to himself or herself or someone they know.

Most insights will generate an "aha" moment. But if you're still not sure, compare it to the following list of what is not a real insight:

Examples of false insights:

* A description of habits & practices *("My consumer consumes more digital media than TV, e.g., media consumption")*
* A "benefit barrier" about a product or category *("My consumer doesn't buy the product because it is too expensive")*
* A superficial or obvious observation *("I want my clothes to be clean"; "I buy perfumes because they smell good")*
* A list of data and facts about the consumer *("Thirty-two-year-old mother of two who lives in the suburbs")*

If the insight you wrote falls into one of these categories, keep working on it. None of the examples above offer a strong emotional connection that is worth resolving. They are also not very distinctive and are rather obvious, which won't make for a great insight.

BENEFIT

The B in IBI stands for benefit. What is a benefit? It represents the promise the brand makes to the consumer about what the brand and product or service will do for them. Consumers buy benefits not product features. So the benefit should give a meaningful reason for the consumer to choose the brand over other alternatives in the market.

A brand's benefit will likely stem from a unique point of difference in the brand equity pyramid. Recall these are the benefits that set the brand apart from competition. It can also be the brand promise articulation that can work as a core brand benefit. These benefits should be relevant to the brand's target. They should rank really high on the list of benefits that are truly important to the target consumer in the category your brand plays in.

Recall from Step 2 of the Star Brand Model that unique benefits can be functional to connect with the mind or emotional to connect with the heart. Functional benefits will speak about the utility of the product. Emotional benefits capture the feeling of owning and experiencing the product.

Self Actualization

Red Bull helps you to push
the boundaries every day

Belonging

Heineken boosts any social setting

Physiological

Trojan Pure Ecstasy improves intimacy through
revolutionary smoothness inside and out

Brand Benefits

*Unique benefits can be functional to connect with the mind
or emotional to connect with the heart.*

Examples of Functional and Emotional Benefits:

* Trojan Pure Ecstasy improves intimacy through revolutionary smoothness inside and out (Physiological)
* Samsonite bags have superior durability (Functional)
* Dyson vacuums never lose suction (Functional)
* GEICO helps you save money on your insurance (Practical/ Savings)
* Little Caesar's Pizza is pre-made, so it's always ready. (Ease)
* Heineken boosts any social setting (Emotional)
* Hyundai Santa Fe gives you confidence to transport your family safely (Emotional/Safety)
* Hilton offers a variety of luxury experiences unique to each destination (Exclusivity)
* Microsoft Office offers continuous support and services anytime, anywhere (Dependability)
* Canon gives you power to see things differently (Self Actualization)
* Red Bull helps you to push the boundaries every day (Self Actualization)

The benefit for the brand or new product included in an advertising brief should strive to be positive and reinforce the brand association. The benefit that you choose for your advertising should also be distinctive to ensure the advertising has a higher likelihood of breaking through the clutter in the market. A strong brand benefit will imply superiority, one that consumers don't think they can find from other brands. This is particularly important for new products. Ask yourself whether the benefit that you are offering consumers is really worth buying and spending advertising development and media dollars on.

IDEA

The last I in IBI stands for idea. A creative idea is the transformation of the communication strategy into a compelling and interesting expression (often a state-ment accompanied with a visual representation) to be executed in an advertising format across marketing touch points. The idea results from a brilliant intersec-tion between a human insight and a brand's benefit. The combination of insight and benefit is what gives birth to a distinctive idea. Benefits need a strong insight to transform into a powerful idea that is relevant to the target consumer. Ulti-mately, an idea that builds the brand is the main deliverable that a brand manager expects from the advertising agency he or she hired.

The idea shouldn't be confused with the ad itself. The idea is the articulation of the insight and benefit of a brand. An ad in any form—TV, print, or digital—is just an execution of an idea. For example, Dove's campaign for real beauty has many different executions including the famous video that went viral on wom-en's sketches or the Camera Shy example whose insight we just studied. There is a broader idea behind all of those executions, which is that Dove recognizes that a woman's authentic beauty is wonderful. You can have a brilliant idea that is exe-cuted poorly, but you can rarely have a brilliant execution that didn't stem from a breakthrough idea. So the money is in the idea. Brand managers in their market-ing capacity should be able to tell apart strong from bad ideas, help articulate the idea, and caress it all the way through excellent execution and launch into market.

Ideas can be executed as part of an existing advertising campaign or inde-pendently. An advertising campaign is a creative platform that lives over time and allows several ideas and ad executions to be born to cover multiple product offerings. Campaigns typically speak about the top of the pyramid—brand ideal or brand promise—whereas individual ideas talk about a specific point of differ-ence or new product. Both campaign and independent ideas need to be routed in a strong insight that connects to consumer; the difference is only whether you want to talk to the consumer about what your brand stands for as a whole or a specific benefit or product you want to hone in on.

Executing an idea as part of a campaign will follow the campaign's consistent glue, which could range from music and taglines to stylistic treatment and con-sistent format. This consistency will likely make the ad stronger and help deliver more "halo" to the total brand. However, campaigns don't come easy. They take time to build and oftentimes strong independent brand ideas can give birth to a longstanding campaign. When you have one, ideas for new advertising come easier as they already have a platform to stand on.

One of the most famous campaigns in advertising history is the "Think Different" campaign from Apple. The campaign embodies the brand's ideal of self-expression and challenging the status quo. The campaign was briefed by Steve Jobs as an initiative to renew Apple's brand image when he regained control of the company in the nineties. Rumor has it that Jobs gave only seventeen days to the agency to come up with an idea and executions. That is not a long time! Nonetheless, the agency delivered. The campaign launched in 1998 and became instantly famous with its TV commercial and print ad that featured black and white video footage of significant historical people of the past, including Albert Einstein, Martin Luther King, Jr., John Lennon, Mahatma Gandhi, and Amelia Earhart, among many others. The TV commercial ends with an image of a young girl, opening her closed eyes, as if to see the possibilities before her. Here is the heart and mind grabbing script from the TV spot.

"Here's to the crazy ones. The misfits. The rebels. The troublemakers. The round pegs in the square holes. The ones who see things differently. They're not fond of rules. And they have no respect for the status quo. You can quote them, disagree with them, glorify or vilify them. About the only thing you can't do is ignore them. Because they change things. They push the human race forward. And while some may see them as the crazy ones, we see genius. Because the people who are crazy enough to think they can change the world, are the ones who do."

Simply beautiful. Iconic. You get the chills and are inspired to "Think Different". Who wouldn't want to buy an Apple product after watching that ad? A very effective campaign to communicate what Apple stands for in the form of an idea. The campaign was not only masterfully executed but it also became the ongoing creative platform for the brand. You might argue that this platform gave birth to all Apple advertising. Even the "Silhouettes" campaign for the Apple iPod launch can be considered an idea execution of the same campaign that encourages self-expression. The essence of the idea of "Think Different" and the use of iconic imagery with high design sensibility still holds. An idea can come from the same

Apple's "Silhouettes" campaign from the original "Think Different" creative platform.

creative platform but can be brought to life in many different ways, especially for new products that will likely need to show new benefits or features.

IBI IN ACTION

To put the concept of IBI in action let's look at the very famous "Priceless" campaign from MasterCard with the tagline, "There are some things money can't buy. For everything else, there's MasterCard." This campaign has been running for almost seventeen years now and has run in over 110 countries.[4] Rather than exclusivity, or status, or the accumulation of stuff, this campaign positions Master-Card as an enabler to the more important things in life. This is a distinct positioning versus competition in the credit card market.

Through research, the MasterCard team discovered that the target consumer was really more interested in building the relationships and special moments that they could have with the people they care about than buying and accumulating a lot of things.[5] That insight married with MasterCard's benefit of wanting to help enable people's lives gave birth to the campaign. The campaign has been executed across multiple effective ad ideas to support different initiatives like holidays, special offers, local market activities, and special services, among others.

for everything else there's *MasterCard*

Creating a campaign that spans a decade and spawned countless imitators: Priceless.

Priceless Campaign Analysis

- **Insight:** Life isn't about what I buy, but about the relationships I have with the people I care most about and the special moments I can share with them.
- **Benefit:** MasterCard enables your life so you can focus on what matters
- **Idea:** Mastercard enables priceless moments.
- **Campaign:** Priceless
- **Tagline:** "There are some things money can't buy. For everything else, there's MasterCard."

As you can see from both campaign examples reviewed, both the "Think Different" from Apple and "Priceless" campaign from MasterCard have stood the test of time and given birth to several independent idea executions. That makes them strong and effective campaigns. Both of these campaigns stem from deep insights married to the overall brand positioning.

CARLING BLACK LABEL CASE STUDY

To wrap up all our IBI learning, let's talk about beer. One of my favorite examples of strong IBI —insights, benefits, and ideas—coming together seamlessly is the "Be the Champion Coach" campaign for Carling Black Label, a South African beer. I want to go in-depth into this case study for two main reasons. First, it is an exceptional example of a golden insight giving birth to an award-winning campaign. Second, its main vehicle of execution was mobile, not the traditional TV spot. Other digital tools and entertainment marketing also played a key role in the idea amplification. In the new marketing era, breakthrough marketing is all about finding the strongest ideas that can work well in any medium. Then select the right mediums to amplify the idea further with the particular advantage the medium offers. To learn more about the advertising brief behind this campaign, I interviewed Lynne Gordon,[6] general manager of BrandTone South Africa, one of the partner agencies behind the campaign along with Ogilvy Cape Town and many others. This is the story of how the campaign came about:

The Carling Black Label brand team and the agency went out on a routine journey to talk to their male core target about their passion points. Since South African men are really passionate about soccer, the team decided to dig deeper in this passion point in particular. They asked questions like: What do you like most about soccer? How do you feel about your favorite soccer team? How and when do you talk about soccer with your friends? The passion for soccer was really obvious. That wasn't an insight per se, so the team dug deeper asking more pointed questions to unleash some consumer tensions, for example: What keeps you up at night about South African soccer? Anything that frustrates you? Boom! That is when tensions and frustration language started to surface and give shape to a possible insight.

While the passion for soccer was obvious in the conversation with consumers, there was a deeper tension in the topic that was frustrating them. It was the sentiment about the coaches from their favorite soccer teams: Orlando Pirates and Kaizer Chiefs. The coaches were disconnected with the local flavor of South African soccer. The fans believed they knew their soccer clubs better than the coaches and could do a better job than them. But shouting from the stands at the

"Be the Champion Coach" was an idea born of a unique insight coupled with a strong benefit.

game or from their couch, their voices went unheard. That was an insight worth going after.

The team, proud of the insight they found, was still at the research facility when they immediately started to place calls back to the creative teams and also to the owners of the soccer teams. Carling Black Label is all about making ordinary men feel like champions, and this insight into the frustration men were feeling gave the platform to do just that—it enabled South African soccer fans to have a voice, to be the champion coach. The creative team smartly married the insight they found with Carling Black Label's positioning of male empowerment to create the "be the champion coach" idea. This idea perfectly solved the target's frustration with the coaches' lack of connection to the local flavor and associated the brand positively with solving this need.

To bring the idea to life, Carling Black Label organized a live match where the two favorite and rival teams would play and the consumers could "Be the coach" by selecting players and making live substitutions during a game simply with their mobile phones. Each Carling Black Label had a special code that allowed them to participate. The beer unlocked the opportunity to be the coach.

This campaign was a breakthrough for the beer category and possibly the most successful mobile promotion in South Africa to date. Carling Black Label's market share increased instantly as votes were linked to sales—one beer, one vote. In the first year the campaign launched, the promotion cast more than 20 million votes during the twelve weeks it lasted. Also, tickets for the historic live match set new records. Research metrics demonstrated high engagement, excitement, and participation, increased positive association with brand attributes and sales resulted ahead of category trends.

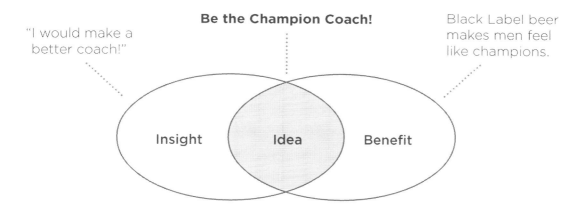

Be the Champion Coach!

"I would make a better coach!"

Black Label beer makes men feel like champions.

Insight   Idea   Benefit

If we apply the IBI framework to this case, this is what it would look like:

- **Insight:** Every man believes he can do a better job than the coach. But shouting from the stands or his couch, his voice goes unheard.
- **Brand Benefit:** Carling Black Label beer enables ordinary men to feel like champions
- **Idea:** Carling Black Label lets you be the coach of your favorite soccer team
- **Campaign:** Be the champion coach

The insight is strong. We clearly see that frustration with coaches is a universal human truth of many passionate fans. It is real in many other countries and it even applies to other sports beyond soccer. But at first it wasn't obvious. It took going deeper in understanding frustrations that surrounded the soccer passion point. The insight also carries a strong emotion that connects with the heart and mind of the consumer, especially as it stems from one of their passion points. There was also a clear tension worth resolving, consumers thought they could do a better job than the current coaches. In this case, Carling Black Label was the right brand to solve the tension with their male empowerment brand promise. This case study proves that once you find the right insight, it can girth birth to a whole marketing campaign. That is the power of a brilliant insight.

The benefit of men empowerment is the brand promise of Carling Black Label. It articulates what the brand can do for the consumer. It is also a higher order benefit consistent with Carling Black Label's positioning as a premium beer. The benefit drives differentiation for the brand in the market place and supports its overall equity of being a Champion brand.

The idea of "Carling lets you be the coach" is clear and distinctive. A perfect marriage of insight and benefit. The Carling team successfully married a strong insight they gathered from their target and married it with the brand's core benefit. Soccer simply happened to be the connecting passion point back to the consumer that allowed the idea to be executed in a very relevant way. Given the success of the campaign, Carling's association with soccer and sporting events in turn became a long-term communication platform for the brand. The following year Carling made the campaign bigger and better, driving not only sales but also with the help of executional consistency, and continued to strengthen the brand's equity and awareness among South African consumers.

The Carling brand team and agency were able to create this wonderful campaign because they understood well their target and their deep life passions and frustrations. Please note that it was not about beer, it was about a bigger life passion point. The team was also crystal clear what Carling Black Label should stand for in the hearts and minds of consumers. That thorough level of brand strategy development and understanding is what you achieve by successfully completing Step 2 and 3 from the Star Brand Model. The output of Step 3 is a strong idea well communicated that builds the brand by creating stronger preference among consumers and more sales of the product, just like the "Be the champion coach" did for Carling Black Label and South African soccer.

HOW IDEAS ARE BUILT — THE BRIEF

Advertising is an art with a consumer-desired response in mind. Advertising offers in the form of an idea the creative transformation of a brand benefit married with a clever way in or relevant human insight. An ad agency executive once told me that, "advertising is a presentation business." I find that very true. Advertising agencies are in the business of selling ideas. They have teams of account people, strategy, and creatives to build the ideas and sell them effectively to clients. Clients, like brand managers, hire advertising agencies to come up with ideas that will persuade consumers to buy their brand.

The most critical talent in an advertising agency is "the creatives." Creative professionals that work in advertising agencies are artists that come up with beautiful and thought-provoking communication for a brand. They are coveted like artists at the agencies, and they often move around from agency to agency in search of bigger brands, better clients, and an overall better creative culture. Therefore, the quality of the ideas you get will be really linked to the type of creatives that work in your advertising assignment.

The starting point of the advertising development process is an advertising brief that the client provides as the request and contract for creative work. Crafting the advertising brief is the responsibility of the brand manager. To create the brief, the brand manager should be very clear on the brand promise and target consumer. Without a brand strategy, a brand's message will lack distinctness, focus, and persuasion, critical characteristics of business-building communication.

To write a solid brief, the brand manager should consult with other people in his or her team including but not limited to other marketers, consumer research experts, the research and development group, and the strategic planner from the agency. The content of the brief will typically require ample strategy discussions and deep understanding of the consumer, all often linked to a specific product or service initiative to grow the business. The brief is considered a brand's communication strategy document. It also becomes the common basis upon which to evaluate the creative work when it comes back from the agency.

Great advertising requires a great brief. It should be clear, inspiring, and simple. There should be a clear challenge for the advertising to solve. Simplicity will get you better creative work, faster. Simplicity leaves room for creative brilliance, which is really what you want from your agency. But simple isn't easier. It takes time to craft a good brief. It is not a document that is written in one or two days, unless you want that type of quality back from the agency. Poorly crafted strategies are typically the number one problem associated with ineffective advertising. You should take the time to write a brief you are proud of.

Advertising briefs will all differ from companies and advertising agencies, but at a minimum, the brief should include five core components:

Core Components of an Advertising Brief

* **Project description.** It includes the business objectives and specific deliverables.
* **A challenge that is worth pursuing.** It should be exciting and capture the desired consumer response that will solve the brand challenge.
* **Target consumer definition.** If you have a profile, include it as well.
* **A well-crafted communication strategy.** One that captures the essence of the message you want to communicate in the form of insight and benefit. It should be consistent with your brand strategy and equity pyramid.
* **Brand assets.** Considerations or guidelines for the agency to use when executing the idea. This will drive brand consistency.

The two most critical components that will get creatives excited and inspired are the challenge and the communication strategy. This is the core of the brief and what will increase your chances of landing a strong idea. The crafting of these statements will require some creativity on the brand manager's part as well.

A Challenge Worth Going After

Advertising agencies are hired to creatively solve a business challenge. The challenge in the brief should be bold and clearly articulate the end state of the brand or the desired change in consumer behavior. The articulation of the challenge will vary from brief to brief and can be anchored in different types of business challenges. For example, a specific brand challenge could be overcoming consumers' reluctance in purchasing a new product, often referred to as trial barrier. In the Sport Club Recife example, the challenge for that brief could have been, "Encourage people to willingly donate their organs." For specific initiatives like new products, the challenge could be around creating awareness of the new product launch or it could be a total brand initiative that seeks to communicate its ideal and overall promise.

Think about the challenge your communication should overcome. Similar to the Vision Trajectory exercise, you can use language such as "Take the brand from X state to Y state." It could also be applied to the consumer as, "Get the target consumer from doing X to Y" or to the category as, "Transform the category from X to Y." Finally, make sure the articulation is clear and exciting and worth going after. You want the agency receiving the brief to be willing to sign up for the challenge with passion.

Communication Strategy: Insight + Benefit

Advertising agencies solve the challenge in the brief by creatively transforming the brand strategy into an idea. The ideas the agency will develop should be rooted in the communication strategy that is included in the advertising brief. The communication strategy gives the creative team the essence of the brand communication to first transform into an idea, which is then followed by a specific creative execution for TV spots, print, radio ads, digital ads, etc. To give birth to an idea, you need to define two critical communication strategy components:

A breakthrough human insight receives "head nods" and has a tension worth resolving. It should ideally come from your target consumer. Superior brand benefit that solves the insight tension and the consumer need should stem from the benefits in your equity pyramid.

As we saw in the MasterCard example, it's the intersection of insight and benefit that will give birth to the idea. That is the magic that you are paying the advertising agency to do.

All of the other components in the brief such as project description, executions, and brand assets to use will provide specificity to the advertising executions. These will become more important once you, the client, purchases an idea and after thorough evaluation and specific advertising executions of the idea are discussed.

EVALUATING ADVERTISING

So you invested precious time in getting the brief right. You hired a great agency to work on the brief and return with ideas. How do you know whether the ideas that you review will be effective in market? The reality is that you will not know whether your advertising is successful until you see its effect in market with either sales or increased product awareness. However, you can increase the chances of your advertising being effective in market prior to producing the final executions via thorough evaluation of the ideas.

Advertising should be considered a business building activity, if the advertising does not generate the desired consumer response, it will be an ineffective investment. Never forget that strong creative is the number-one driver of media's return on investment (ROI). If the ad is ineffective, you are wasting the dollars invested in media to put that particular message on air. Your advertising should be driving your brand's benefit in a distinctive way that persuades consumers to buy.

Effective adverting is persuasive and connects with the heart and mind of consumers. An ad, a specific execution of a creative idea, is effective when it persuades the consumer to take action with respect to the brand e.g. buying the brand, talking about it, yearning for more information. Additionally, effective advertising creates strong and positive brand associations and contributes to building stronger brand equity over time. This is consistent with the idea that one of the brand manager's goals is to create a stronger affinity with the brand every time a consumer is exposed to a branded message.

During the advertising development process, your best bet in landing effective advertising is to properly evaluate the first set of ideas presented and select only the best ideas to continue developing specific advertising executions. Then you can work with the advertising agency to make the creative work and the idea bigger and better. You can also choose to expose it to consumers in research to get some reactions. Skilled brand managers have the ability to take advertising from good to great and also tell apart strong ideas from poor ideas.

How advertising is evaluated varies from company to company, industry to industry, and from marketer to marketer. There are also nuances for each particular category the brand belongs to that are important to evaluate early on in the advertising for it to be effective. For example, in categories like pharmaceutical products that are heavily regulated, there are certain advertising formats, features, and treatments that are important to deliver on marketing executions to meet category conventions and also be effective in the market place.

Each marketing organization has their own set of principles on how to evaluate it based on previous executions, category expertise, or even proprietary research. Every brand manager also has his or her own way of evaluating advertising. This skill strengthens with the more advertising you evaluate, create, and launch. Doing a lot of advertising and seeing successes and failures over time will calibrate your marketing compass and ability to build big ideas.

When evaluating advertising, there are a couple of questions you can use to dissect the idea and also help determine whether it meets the characteristics of what makes advertising effective. Ultimately, the intent of the advertising is to be effective in persuading the consumer to buy. Answering a consistent set of questions helps diagnose the strength of each creative submission. This is a practical exercise to do as well with any ad that you watch as a consumer. If you train yourself to evaluate advertising creative expressions through this lens, you will become better at telling apart poor from great advertising. It's a powerful exercise.

Key questions to ask when reviewing ideas:

First time you look at it, do you like it?
When I look at advertising for the first time, I evaluate it as a consumer first. After

all, marketers are humans and consumers too. One of my advertising mentors used to tell me "the first time you see an idea or an ad, is the last time you will see it as a consumer." From then on you will look at it as a marketer.

Your first gut reaction is really valuable so that is the first reaction that you should record. I typically even use the old tactic of happy face, frowny face or neutral to get my gut reaction recorded the first time I see it. This is also typically a good measure whether you want to see the advertising again, which tends to be a sign of advertising effectiveness. Finally, if the idea that I review for the first time is not clear, and I give a frowny face to, it gives me the red flag that I need to ask more questions about the idea to properly evaluate it. Of course this is something I simply write on my evaluation notes and not for the agency to see.

What benefit is the idea selling?

When reviewing advertising, it is helpful to have the brief submitted to the agency as evaluation reference. The idea should be about the benefit included on the brief. Remember that for advertising to be effective, it should communicate the benefit in a very distinctive way, typically with an interesting twist or even a reframe of the benefit. Distinctiveness is necessary for the idea and the ad to break through the clutter. If the idea doesn't sell the benefit, please don't buy it. The Carling "Be the champion coach" idea does a great job of bringing to the brand's benefit of male empowerment to life.

What emotion does the idea trigger?

Effective advertising connects with the heart and the mind of consumers, i.e., emotionally and rationally. Did you get any goose bumps as you listened to the idea? What emotion did the idea trigger? Does it make you feel good about the brand? Does it evoke a positive or negative feeling? Was there a strong hook? Typically the insight is what will help connect with the consumer's heart and mind and carry the tension and emotion in an idea. Evaluate how the insight is playing a role in the idea. The Sport Club Recife and Dove examples do a great job of triggering strong visceral emotions with the execution whether it is the love for your soccer team that makes you want to donate or the realization that you hide from the camera because you stopped thinking you are beautiful.

Does it build your brand?

Every advertising execution you bring to market needs to pay homage to your brand. Strong branding and consistent portrayal of the brand's character will pay dividends to the brand equity. How many times have you watched ads that you find interesting but you don't remember which brand it was for? It is possible that the drama overtook the role of the product or the branding cues were weak. Unfortunately, an ad that can't recall which brand it is for is wasted money for the advertiser. Make sure, especially during the production phase of the advertising, that the execution is undeniably linked to your brand. This is what the consumer will register and you want to recall next time he or she goes to the store.

Your brand value or equity should increase because of the great advertising you have in market. The MasterCard Priceless campaign does a great job of building the brand; every time a "Priceless" ad execution runs around the world it is reinforcing and building the equity of the MasterCard brand.

Is the idea media neutral?

It is common that ideas are presented already in execution formats, e.g., print ad, Facebook post, TV script. However, the idea that you select shouldn't be dependent of the medium it is presented on. A strong idea is flexible enough that you can imagine it living across multiple consumer touch points. Focus on evaluating the idea and its articulation first, not its executions.

The idea can come to life slightly differently across those mediums using the uniqueness that each vehicle offers. It is not intended to be a "copy and paste" of the idea on print, in-store, or on TV but the executions should consistently execute the idea. If you pick an idea that is too dependent on one particular execution in one medium or is the only way the idea works, it is possible that you are falling in love with the specific execution tactic or the media vehicle. If you do find a brilliant execution that you don't want to pass on, push yourself and the agency to articulate what the idea is independent of the medium execution. If the idea is really big, you should be able to articulate it and in this exercise also expand it across touch points. Finally, the idea should be media neutral, because the mediums that you choose to execute it on should be guided by the consumer receptivity to the message and the medium. We will go in depth on media in the upcoming chapter. For now keep in mind that you shouldn't buy ad executions; buy strong ideas.

Answering these questions helps you articulate why the particular idea or advertising you are evaluating works or why it doesn't and whether you should pursue it, or evolve it and bring it to market. The objective of evaluating advertising thoroughly is that you increase the quality of the idea and its chances of being effective in market. A more thorough evaluation process for ideas requires some practice however. As you are practicing using the evaluation exercise several times, it will become natural to evaluate advertising. If you train yourself to always use it you will be able to more consistency identify the ideas that have the highest potential.

Now that you know how ideas are built and how you can go about creating IBI and a communication strategy, I challenge you to do two things:

First, go back and look at all the briefs you have ever worked on. Rewrite them with the principles we studied. Would you have landed potentially a stronger idea than what you currently have? If you have never written a brief, write one for the brand you love. Start playing with these principles. Craft a challenge worth going after for your brand and use the IBI Venn diagram framework to see how the components connect and the possible intersections between insight and benefit could work.

Second, start evaluating advertising on your own to strengthen your marketing skills. It will help you build a strong idea evaluation compass. You can do either just while watching TV, or search for your favorite spot. See how well it does versus these criteria. If the ad made you love the brand more and motivated you to buy, it will probably get "passing colors" on all these evaluation questions and a happy face.

Advertising Evaluation Guide

Here are some additional helpful questions to use when you are evaluating an idea or advertising execution:

- What is the ad's main idea? Is it clear?
- Is there a human insight with a tension that the brand resolves?
- What is the benefit? Is the idea about the benefit included in the brief?
- Who is the advertising for? Is it relevant to your target consumer?
- Does it connect with the consumer's heart and mind? What emotion or connection does it trigger?
- Is it distinctive? Have you heard it before? Does it make you think about the benefit in a new way?
- Does it pay homage to the top of the Equity pyramid?
- Is the idea dependent of one particular medium? Is it flexible enough to travel across touch points?

Understanding Media

"Half my advertising is wasted, I just don't know which half."

— John Wanamaker, American Retailer, (1838-1922)

By now you know what your brand is all about, the target you are going after, and you have an idea to advertise your appealing product. The next question is, how will you make the idea travel to reach the consumers? The answer is by developing a well-crafted media strategy and selecting the right media vehicles.

   Media is the primary method brands use to get their branding and messaging in front of the right people in the right place and at the right time. Given this, for many of the world's top brands, paid media is the largest expenditure of the company's marketing budget, with some brands such as McDonald's spending nearly $1 billion per year[1] in the US alone on media. For consumer goods giants who own many household brands, that number skyrockets to upwards of $8-9 billion globally.[2]

The process of media planning entails selecting the best media vehicles to reach the consumer and budgeting for the amount of media that you need to reach the desired media objectives such as awareness. As a brand manager, media planning was probably one of my favorite tasks. Building a communication and media plan is really when a brand manager is placing bets with real money. Selecting the right media will make your marketing more effective. Selecting the wrong media vehicle or buying a lot of media for an ineffective message will deflate your return on investment in media and marketing dollars. If this happens, you not only have to deal with the impact of having less sales this year but also you won't have a strong investment case to make at the upcoming marketing plan year when you are requesting dollars to invest in media.

The goal of this next section is to provide you context to the media landscape and how to strategically use marketing money to help boost your brand's presence against your target consumer.

THE MEDIA LANDSCAPE

The media world is complex and ever-changing. To bring you the latest media insights, I spent some time with Andres Mongrue, a rising star in the media planning and buying world. He works at a media agency that buys media on behalf of major advertising spenders. Day in and day out he works with the realities of the media world, not only the client side but also the actual media companies.

Let's begin by acknowledging the macro influences that impact the complex media landscape that exists today.

Evolution of the Consumer
With advances in technology, information sharing, and the globalization of the traditional consumer, people have become more diverse as individuals. How they consume media has mirrored this changing reality and requires advertisers to become laser focused in their targeting strategies. A blanket target definition of "Women aged eighteen to forty-nine in the US" must now become "Women

aged eighteen to forty-nine interested in beauty and fashion-related content." These consumers will have a particular media consumption behavior. A beauty aficionado may subscribe to five to ten monthly beauty magazines to stay up-to-date while a sports enthusiast would more likely spend that money on premium sports packages as part of their cable television choices.

Proliferation of Media

As consumers have evolved, so too have their choices for consuming content. Today the choices are endless with digital providing more choice so marketers must fight for attention. In the early days of advertising, one commercial on a hit TV show could capture a significant percentage of a brand's target in one fell swoop. Even as recently as the 1980s, a spot in the finale of *M.A.S.H* got you 60 percent of the total US population in one night.[3] Fast forward to the 2000s where the biggest hit show *Friends* got you a little under 30 percent of American eyes. Compare those numbers today where the biggest sitcom of the day, *The Big Bang Theory*, only pulls in around 5 percent of the US population during premiere episodes.[4]

Increasing Media Budgets

Big brands are spending enormous amounts of money to place their ads on TV networks, print magazines, billboards, websites, etc. The media industry itself is a $500 billion global industry.[5] With all this money changing hands and negotiations having higher stakes, media properties needed to consolidate to achieve scale and gain back some of their negotiation power to remain competitive. A TV network like Bravo will be more attractive to advertisers and do much better selling ad space if they come to the table as part of NBCUniversal versus trying to negotiate alone. This consolidation has happened across channels with companies like Time Inc. for print, Google for digital, JCDecaux for out-of-home billboards and Clear Channel for radio, acquiring properties as part of their portfolio. In this landscape, advertisers partner with media agencies that pool their clients' money in an attempt to gain leverage of their own during those negotiations. In its simplest form, media agencies have become the brokers of advertising, negotiating for the best rates on behalf of their portfolio of clients.

Technology

Technology is shaping the media industry significantly. It has been a major driver of change by shifting how advertisers and consumers buy, consume, and share content. From a consumer standpoint, the biggest changes have resulted in a proliferation of choice. What started with DVR and the ability to pause live TV to re-watch at your convenience has evolved to On-Demand content delivered at your fingertips through any device with an Internet connection at any time. In this new world, consumers can choose what content they want to consume whenever it is convenient for them and across any device they choose be it a phone, tablet, or TV screen.

For marketers, technology is shaking things up as well, increasing the importance of relevancy. In a world where consumers can avoid your ad with the click of a "skip" button, switch tabs on a web browser or simply thumb-scroll over your ad on a mobile phone, advertisers must find new ways to break through. With things shifting online, marketers can now take advantage of that same technology consumers are using to understand their behaviors across devices, ensuring that the message delivered is tailored to that individual's specific needs or interests, in turn benefiting both the advertiser and the consumer. This type of capability has sparked a new demand for data collection and analytics more than ever before to improve consumer targeting. Additionally, new automated media buying tools allow advertisers to only purchase the "impressions" or eyeballs of consumers that are relevant to the brand or more likely to be receptive to a particular message. This match-up of data collection with more sophisticated media buying technology is allowing the delivery of the right message on the right device to the right consumer at the right time in an automated way.

TODAY'S MEDIA CHOICES

In order to think about how to use media to your advantage as a brand manager, you must first understand your choices available today. The number of media channels is vast and it quickly becomes difficult to fully grasp the full range of media consumers are using, however there are some key channels that every brand manager needs to be familiar with as part of their marketing mix. Additionally, how you use these channels can vary from the industry standard to the most custom of executions. We'll go into a few examples below to help illustrate some of these differences.

Television

Despite all of the changes the industry has seen over the past few decades, TV remains king spending-wise. Fifty-eight percent[6] of the nearly $600 billion[7] Global Media Industry comes from television spending. TV is very effective at driving quick and massive reach at very efficient costs. Nearly every major advertiser utilizes TV as an awareness driver, especially when introducing new products. If you think about an advertiser like Ford introducing their newest lineup of cars, you probably think about their high reaching Super Bowl spots or their fall sales promotions where they are clearing out the old models with deep discounts and promotions to prepare for the release of the new models. In both cases, they are targeting in mass and want consumers to be aware of their product or promotion.

Other advertisers such as CPGs (consumer product goods) and confectioners face a different kind of challenge. Their consumers often are not putting as much thought into the brand choices they make so these advertisers need to ensure their brand is top of mind. Continuous TV presence is one of the most effective ways to ensure efficient reach against an audience so that the next time a consumer is looking for toothpaste or gum, that brand comes to mind.

Today, TV also has to compete with other available video content media choices online and in mobile. In the US for example, 2013 marked a pivotal year for time spent with media as time spent with Digital media for the first time surpassed TV.[8] The decline in time spent with TV has continued in to 2014 as video watching habits change, especially among newer generations of consumers.[9] Therefore, TV instead of traditionally being considered as the main or only medium to drive video content, should be now considered as part of a wider set of options, recognizing that it is probably still the best tool for driving mass reach with video content.

TV, as a dominant medium, has a standard format which is what you are probably most familiar with: the TV commercial. The specifications of these can vary across markets; however, the intent is the same. Marketers buy ad space during commercial breaks ranging anywhere from 0:05 seconds to 2:00 minutes, with the 0:15 and 0:30 spots being the most common both globally and in the US. There are, however, custom executions from sponsorships to integrations, which is where brands and media can get very creative. In an effort to differentiate itself and build off of a TV show, actor, or program's equity, some brands will broker media deals to integrate their brand right in to the program.

General Motors made an appeal to a younger audience through a partnership with *Glee* in a 2011 Super Bowl ad.

A great example of this is what General Motors did in 2011 with the up and coming American show, *Glee*. General Motors has an aging customer base and needed to find ways to become relevant with today's audience. *Glee*, a show that had gained popularity from taking songs from the fifties and sixties and popularizing them with today's use was, a perfect match. GM decided that in an effort to better appeal to younger audiences they would create a custom commercial with the cast of *Glee*, taking the classic 1950's Chevy jingle ("See the U-S-A in your Chev-ro-let!") and popularizing it through a modern rendition performed by the cast of *Glee* making it both relevant to their core target and building off of *Glee*'s equity with their young audiences. The deal involved a custom 2:00 commercial appearing immediately after the Super Bowl and right in to a new episode of *Glee*, maximizing on the high numbers of consumers within their target that would make the transition with the network.[10]

Print

Although faced with declining readership and speculation that the industry has turned its back on print, there is still a very strong role for print in many brands' marketing plans. Print can range anywhere from newspaper text classifieds to high-resolution image ads inserted into magazines. Despite the readership declines, print in many markets can drive significant reach against specific demographic groups such as young females interested in beauty and fashion or adults who rely on their morning newspaper for information. In global markets where Internet has not reached its full potential in terms of market penetration, newspaper and print can play an even larger role as it is often still a primary source of news and information. Aside from the reach benefits that marketers should consider when building a media plan, there is also the consideration of the environment of something like a magazine. Magazines are often cited as one of the more trusted mediums,[11] and one where a consumer's attention is highly focused to the medium. Think about the ads in a magazine versus the ads you may see on TV. Often times, especially for fashion ads, the ads are almost as important as the magazine content.

Now think about TV where aside from a few occasions, such as the Super Bowl, you could be passively experiencing the ads. You might be using this time to grab a snack, go to the bathroom, or finish up your conversation with a friend. Just like with TV, print has standard ad types as well as custom. Within newspapers, there are several sizes and color types that ads can be placed in. Most common are the standard box ads for which an advertiser buys space adjacent to content. Ideally, most advertisers will want to align with content related to their brand equity or to content related to the brand, but this can depend. For example, a bank may want to be in the finance section whereas an auto may want to advertise in the Sunday paper where all the deals are aggregated to announce their new promotional financing offers on a new car. Within magazines you most often see what is called a page four-color bleed, or P4CB. This is just an industry term to explain it is a full page, full color ad that bleeds to the end of the page.

Custom executions are where print can really get interesting. There is often more flexibility in integrating directly with the content, and because themes and editorial calendars are aligned far in advance, you get to see some very interesting and effective executions within print. Take for example a fashion retailer that wants to showcase its newest line. Often times, print publications have relationships with influencers in the fashion industry that they can partner with brands to create custom content "advertorials" where the product is being talked about and endorsed. The goal is to seem as authentic as possible, noting that legally advertisers must reveal on the page that it is a paid advertisement. It's a great way to really deliver product information or benefits in a way that is both beneficial to the consumer as well as the advertiser.

Another example is what *Newsweek* did in 2012 with several advertisers. For their *Mad Men* edition magazine, they offered an opportunity to advertisers to theme their ads in a retro style to align with the *Mad Men* theme throughout. The result was a highly talked about edition where the ads themselves became part of the content.[12]

Allstate's "Mad Men" ad.

Out-of-Home (OOH)

What is the first city that comes to mind when you hear about out-of-home advertising? If you've ever been to New York City, you probably instantly have images of Times Square's massive billboards that are some of the most viewed ads in the world with over 39 million people passing through annually.[13] Even if you haven't, it's likely still one of the top spots you think about when it comes to OOH advertising due to its media coverage around the world. OOH, much like TV and print, is one of the traditional mass advertising vehicles that works to drive awareness for brands.

The traditional placement for an OOH ad is a billboard where an advertiser's branding message is printed and placed on the board for a specific duration of time. You've probably seen these while on the highway in many cities. One of the major issues with these billboards is just like all mediums, clutter is becoming a problem and consumers are tuning them out. Standing out through a unique placement or creative idea is key for OOH to work well. OOH has evolved to provide opportunities for more custom executions as well as digital versions that can be sold with more flexibility. A great example of both a digital billboard as well as one that has been custom modified for an advertisers needs is a recent British Airways campaign in which technology enabled the boards to activate when a plane was detected overhead. The digital boards had an image of a child who would stand up and begin to point at the plane, which then created a very disruptive ad that really stood out and grabbed attention. Whether you're buying a standard placement or a technology enabled board, in OOH bigger is often better to try to get as many eyeballs as possible.

Radio

There is a misconception that radio advertising is ineffective because it's old. Just like any medium, it is important to understand its role and then identify whether it should be included in your media mix. Radio should always be considered in terms of your audience's behavior towards the medium. For many advertisers, radio is a challenge due to its lack of visuals. All the other channels have prominent visuals at the center of the ad's strength. Also, many brands rely on visual cues to communicate their brand equity, whether through logos, colors, fonts, or characters further making radio advertising a challenge. That said, radio can still be a powerful tool in its ability to geo target as well as to get people to act quickly. Think about when you are listening to the radio. You're probably in your car on your way to someplace. Radio has the ability to reach you while you are on the go travelling and, if utilized correctly, can get people to adjust their destination. Let's say you are a car dealership targeting consumers in the market for a new car and you want them to come to your lot during your promotional sale happening right now. You can run your radio ads in an efficient manner only to people in your market who are already out and about. If you're in the market for a car, you're probably stopping at multiple dealerships during your search, so hearing an ad for a new special promotion while you're going from one dealership to another can easily sway you to add one more dealership to your list.

Put simply, radio is an effective tactical tool for promotional or location-based activities where you want to get people somewhere. It can often be used to help promote PR events and get more attention to a brand's local activities.

Another important use of standard radio is leveraging radio personalities as endorsements. If you're targeting an audience with a high affinity towards a certain radio personality or that personality has a strong influence on the audience, an endorsement can really convince. In the United States we often see this with Hispanic and African American audiences who have passion for music and look to DJs as key influencers.

Digital

We've gone through most of the traditional channels, and I've left digital for last, given its impact on consumer behavior and all of the other mediums. As we mentioned in the TV section, consumers are spending more time with digital media. Technology and the Internet have enabled all of the traditional channels to be moved online with great speed and choice for consumers. For advertisers, this has opened up a new world of targeting capabilities, tracking, and opportunities to connect directly with consumers. Whether video content on a computer versus on a TV, print editorial on a tablet, or radio on a mobile phone, the Internet has made content readily available through a variety of platforms. With all the flexibility of the Internet, there are a variety of ways to advertise online. The most common ways are search, display, social, and video.

Search in its simplest form is putting your brand in front of someone looking for information related to your product. For example, if someone searches for "dresses" on Google, a retailer could pay to have their advertisement displayed as a potential search result so that the consumer can think of this retailer as part of their consideration as they continue searching for dresses. This form of advertising is often considered one of the most effective given the consumer is actively searching, thus likely more receptive. The key is being as relevant as possible by only buying search ads when your product or website is truly delivering on what the consumer is looking for.

Display and video are the next largest methods of advertising online. These are essentially the equivalent of TV commercials and out-of-home billboards. In the case of display, advertisers can purchase banners that appear on a page. By leveraging various targeting methods, advertisers can buy ads that only reach those people deemed most likely to be interested in their advertised product (this is can be based on custom research or deep understanding of the target segment). Digital video works the same way but finds ways to serve up video content to consumers. For example, on YouTube sometimes you may come across an ad that you are required to watch before the clip you were looking for can play. This is called a pre-roll, given it comes before the content. There are several variations of this with some being click-to-play or even integrating into a program during commercial breaks much like on TV. Hulu is a great example of taking the TV model and applying it online for quality programming.

One of the greatest advantages of digital is the endless possibility for customization at scale. We discussed many of the different types of more advanced or custom executions from TV integrations to billboards using advanced technology or print leveraging influential content; with digital all of the above is possible but faster and with even more flexibility. Today, within digital websites we see ads that seemingly explode from the page and allow consumers to interact with a brand on a whole new level. For example, when the movie Godzilla released, it launched a Yahoo! takeover where consumers were greeted on the Yahoo! homepage with a video experience that not only displayed the trailer but provided consumers options to find cinema locations, buy tickets, download a ringtone or share the content on their social news feed. Digital is offering customization at scale and companies are racing to see who can innovate fastest.

Customer Relationship Management (CRM)

CRM in its most basic form is, as the name suggests, managing your relationship with your customers, often through a collection of personal data. If you've purchased a car from a dealership sometime before the 2000s you may have received a handwritten note from your salesperson thanking you for your business. Three months later you might have gotten a reminder from the dealership for an oil change with a discount included recommending you get this done at their certified dealership service center. This is the traditional form of CRM that has now mostly evolved to a digital platform consisting of a database of current or perspective customer data and online communication tools such as email to continue the relationship with them. This database can be used as part of a wealth of strategies, such as learning about consumer behavior, cross-selling, trading up, or even positioning current consumers as advocates but the main objective remains the same; CRM databases are intended to manage consumer information with the goal of marketing and selling products or services. So whether an advertiser chooses to send monthly email offers, target new products to current customers through digital banners, learn more about consumers who purchase their products, or look to build an ongoing relationship with consumers via incentives or education, a CRM database can be an effective solution.

Public Relations (PR) and Earned Media

More recently a great deal of public relations has been dedicated to generate earned media, which is the unpaid portion of media. Earned media is any free exposure your brand is given whether through PR media coverage or by consumers sharing your brand. The increasing difficulty for brands to break through, and the emergence of social networks have placed a new priority on finding ways to effectively drive earned media with consumers.

Media Outreach

Though not new, the media outreach approach has evolved over the last decade. Brand managers have always had PR teams that developed relationships with media outlets to pitch stories on new products or innovations in the hopes that the editorial teams at these media houses would pick up this content and run it as news. It is important to note that this is all unpaid editorial work and it is at the sole discretion of the editorial team whether or not to cover the story, and with what angle, and that it is not always guaranteed to be positive. Therefore, PR agencies must work to identify an angle for the brand that makes the news "newsworthy." A media publication is not going to pick up a story that will bore its readers or be irrelevant. Further, the art of media outreach has continued to evolve in today's new digital world. With content "going viral," brands have a new opportunity or angle to get coverage from media outlets based on how "shareable" their content may be. With consumers craving original content, media has placed more emphasis on picking up these kinds of stories, presenting new opportunities for marketers and PR agencies.

Additionally, the best media outreach is timed with paid media—the other media channels we discussed earlier—so that it can build momentum and work hand-in-hand to deliver the most earned or "free" media. Increasingly marketers are asking that their PR and media agencies work hand-in-hand to develop strategies on how to drive the best-earned exposure. Given the importance being placed on the content itself, the creative agency must also be involved so that the content they develop is of interest to both brand consumers and the media. Today's landscape is requiring a more collaborative environment between partner agencies for success.

Blogger Relations

Even with all the changes today, recommendations from key influences are just as important as ever, if not more. With blogs granting individuals instant follower communities, online bloggers have become a new kind of influencers. As a result, via bloggers, a new channel has emerged to "influence" consumers' brand and product choices. Many marketers in the beauty and tech industries for example, rely on relationships with bloggers to gain positive coverage of their products so that the articles and reviews written are positive and distributed through these blogger communities. By demonstrating product benefits, providing exclusive first looks, and educating on points of difference, marketers can help ensure that bloggers understand the product in full when they write their reviews. The goal is a positive endorsement from these influencers and their communities.

Social Media

Most people reading this book will have a Facebook account and many may even have a Twitter, Instagram, or Pinterest account as well. Consumers today look to social media for news, entertainment, trends, etc. so it is an opportunity for brands to become a part of the conversation happening today. The key for brands is to understand their voice in social media and post content that their audience will find interesting and is appropriate for the relationship they want to build. The reward is consumers will share and engage with that content which can be seen by their friends and can become an instant endorsement for the brand.

Brands can also take things a step further by using paid social media to drive scale and advanced targeting. Today several advertising dollars are going to social media as paid media for brands to be part of targeted social conversations. This trend is likely to continue as advertisers are always looking for ways to more effectively connect with consumers as new social media platforms emerge.

CREATING A MEDIA PLAN

Now that you have an overview of the media landscape and choices, we'll walk through the five key steps in building an effective media plan for your brand.

STEP 1: Understanding When & Where Your Consumer Is Most Receptive
An ad for snow tires in Texas in the middle of the summer is clearly a poor choice for a snow tire company for several obvious reasons. However, things are not always this obvious, so marketers need to consider when their target is most receptive to their message to maximize its effectiveness. Receptivity is the understanding of when and where consumers are ready to listen that allows marketers to best deliver their brand message. This requires a solid understanding of your target consumer. Here are some key questions to answer as part of this process about your target consumer:

Key Questions About Your Target Consumer

* What channels does my consumer use most?
* Is my brand message more relevant for certain geographies?
* What channels does my consumer use most to consume the type of information I'm delivering?
* Is there a season or time of day when my brand message will be more relevant—when my consumers are most receptive to my message.
* Are there triggers that get my consumer thinking about the information I'm delivering?

Utilizing third party audience tools such as MRI, TGI, Nielsen, Experian Simmons, or Comscore, can get you some of the answers of these questions. To get even more granular you can consider also conducting qualitative or quantitative studies for your specific brand.

STEP 2: Selecting the Right Media Vehicles

Once you are clear about your consumer receptiveness to media, you can begin to select the right media mix for your particular brand message and communication goal. To create the ideal combination of medium, begin by asking: What is my brand objective and what am I trying to communicate? Understanding what you are trying to communicate should always direct your choices. It is the north star of your media plan. If you are trying to educate a consumer on how your product works, you're going to end up in a different environment or media channel than if your goal is to entertain and engage them. If this question is not answered correctly or is not well defined, it can throw off your entire media plan.

Once you've nailed down your objective, you can begin to select your media vehicles. A great way to narrow them down is first by the frequency of use of the medium by the consumer and then by which mediums are most relevant for your specific message. For example, if your target consumer watches TV frequently but is also a heavy online browser, begin with those vehicle choices. Try to become more granular, such as looking at specific TV channels or websites your consumer is spending time on to maximize how efficiently you can drive reach within that channel by spending your money on those choices. Also, if your audience isn't spending time reading magazines, you can easily look past this media choice for others they are using more frequently.

After frequency of use of the medium, receptivity of the message in it is a strong filter to make the final vehicle selection. Just because your target consumer is spending a lot of time playing online games does not necessarily mean this is the best place to communicate a complicated education message on how to use your new product. If you are a high end retailer that has used this question to determine that certain print magazine titles are highly trusted for fashion choices, you may choose these channels over TV despite TV's higher reach. MRI and primary research are great tools to understand how receptive your consumer is to your message in certain environments. These studies offer insight into things like what channels your consumer trusts most, what mindset they are in, or what channels they go to first when seeking out answers related to your product or category.

STEP 3: Optimizing Each Vehicle

Once you have filtered down potential media vehicles based on the target's medium frequency and receptivity, you should consider how each vehicle can be best used and optimized. With this in mind, additional considerations such as seasonality, geography, and behavior or mindset triggers can make a media plan more precise.

Seasonality and time of day can be great tools for marketers to take advantage of. Depending on a consumer's mindset at the time of message delivery, your ads may be more relevant and impactful than at other times. To answer this question you'll want to study your consumer's behaviors over time. For example, you can look at Google search trends throughout the year to find out when consumers begin looking for holiday gift ideas, which can be extremely useful to a retailer preparing their holiday marketing blitz. Primary qualitative research can also reveal interesting insights that would not have been realized without probing on the consumer journey. You can also use intuition in some cases to determine when your message might be more time relevant. If you manage a fast food brand for example and want to target office workers for lunch options, your advertising should happen around hours when this information is most relevant. An ad that offers "quick and easy food delivery options for the office" at 3 PM, after lunch has passed, won't be as relevant and likely forgotten by the next day versus focusing your campaign to start by 11AM and end at 2 PM which is when lunch decisions are being made.

Geography can also play a role in tailoring your media plan. The receptiveness to a message and the effectiveness of a particular vehicle can change by location, regions, or country considerations. Like the snow tire sale in the Texas example from before, not all geographies are relevant for a particular message. This can apply to restaurant chains only available in certain cities or promotional offers that are only available regionally. A major advertiser who has taken geography into consideration for its media plan is Chick-fil-A, a quick-service US chicken restaurant. Understanding that the vast majority of their stores are in the southeast US, they have leveraged geo-based OOH campaigns heavily. Additionally, they have taken this further through their ongoing partnership with the SEC College Football Sponsorship they have maintained the past few years making effort to locally target where relevant to their stores and core customers.

Another consideration for making your media plan more precise is any behavioral or mental trigger that can make a consumer more receptive to your message. These are often tied to critical moments or life stages affecting a consumer's lives which can happen with age changes, time of year, etc. People can flow in and out of these moments continuously. If you've ever moved to a new apartment or home in the United States, one thing you've probably noticed is that you almost always receive a welcome packet from the US Postal Service, and with it come mailer ads. This is because advertisers such as cable companies, furnishing stores, etc. know that when people move they are likely in a life stage change where they will be making decisions related to cable providers or home furniture. These advertisers have found an effective way to target recent movers and make their products available at a relevant decision time. Digital is beginning to make this more scalable as social media is providing more visibility into these life stages and make targeting more precise. For example, targeting people who recently got engaged, recently moved, or just graduated is now possible through platforms like Facebook. Since media targeting capabilities will no longer be a barrier, the key is to pin point the most critical consumer behaviors or mental triggers that can make your message more relevant.

STEP 4: Determining the Right Budget Level
When it comes time to deciding how much money you want to spend on getting your brand out there, you don't want to fall short by underspending and you don't want to spend too much and waste it. As John Wanamaker alluded to, "What?" "How much?" and "Where?" are all questions that marketers face, and with today's hefty media budgets, a lot is at stake. This is why marketers must take as many pieces of information or input as possible to try and methodically determine their media spending.

Media will likely be taking up a big portion of the marketing budget, so the media budget becomes a critical component of a brand's marketing spend, a cost reflected in the P&L. The truth is there is not a right answer to an exact budget level as it will greatly vary based on the brand objective, the target consumer, the message, the resources available, and the willingness to invest, as well as the category dynamics. Also, budgets can change dramatically year to year. However, with the right inputs and best use of the data available, a brand manager can make choices and determine an optimal budget to accomplish the brand's specific goals. Below we will review two approaches to set the budget for your media.

Budgeting Based on Historical Data
When available, previous market performance for your brand or media spending can be a great starting point to budget for a new marketing plan. Here are some examples of historical data and metrics you can use as benchmarks for media spending:

- **Sales Data:** Past year performance on your own business as well as that of your competition can provide perspective as to the effectiveness of everyone's marketing plan.
- **Ad Spends:** Third party tools such as Nielsen AdViews can help provide directional ideas of where your spending stacks up against the competition if you have previously bought media.
- **Share of Voice (SOV):** Also available in Nielsen AdViews, share of voice determines your share of the total gross rating points (GRPs) vs. your competitors. Primarily used for TV levels, SOV is measuring how much your ad is being shown to the marketplace (not to be confused with reach).
- **Key Performance Indicator (KPI) Studies:** Third party data companies such as Millward Brown are often used to measure campaigns from a behavioral KPI standpoint such as awareness lifts or purchase intent. Reviewing these studies from past campaigns can help identify the most effective channels to prioritize.

- Market Mix Modeling (MMM): Third party analysis firms use regression analysis to determine the return on marketing investment you achieved in past years. These studies can be very expensive, but are used by some of the largest advertisers to get data on which marketing choices are driving the highest return.

- Marketplace data: Actual media costs should be a factor to consider as you set your spend levels.

Marketers rely on media agencies and data companies to look back at the past year's data to help make choices to reach their sales goals for the upcoming year. However, since it is likely you won't always have all of the above data or the resources to hire a media agency or data supplier, by working through the media objective, your consumer understanding, and a few key data points you can still build a sound media budget for your brand.

Budgeting Based on the Sales/Spending Ratio
Whether you have historical data or your have made a set of assumptions, you can also follow a budget setting approach that is based on the sales-to-spend ratio for your particular category. That is the level of media spending that is required to sell the product or service unit of a particular brand.

To explain this budgeting approach, let's use a new car company that we will call the "Lightning Car." We will walk though the different steps this brand used to set its media budget. Lightning Car has a goal of increasing their 2014 US market share of cars from 5 percent of total car sales to 10 percent of all car sales in 2015. Analysts are expecting auto sales to remain flat, so unless Lightning Car can grow the category, bringing in completely new users, it will need to steal share from competition to hit its market share goals.

1. Determine your market sales goal

Using publicly available competitor and first party sales data, Lightning Car was able to determine that there is $100 million worth of car sales annually in the United States, of which $5 million is currently going to Lightning Car. In order to increase their share to 10 percent, they would need to achieve $10 million in sales, meaning their 2015 sales goal is $10 million.

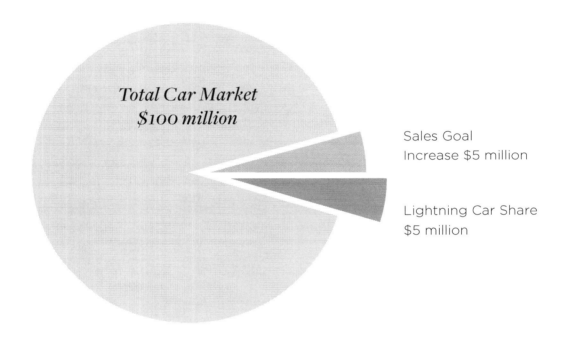

2. Analyze industry trends to set spend-to-sales ratio

With a sales goal set, the next step is to look at industry trends as well as historical data to determine the brand's spend-to-sales ratio. The Lightning Car brand manager, with third party tool, Nielsen AdViews, determined that approximately $40 million was spent on media to help fuel those $100 million in car sales across the category. From this information, we can infer that for every $1 spent on media, $2.50 was earned in car sales last year giving car manufacturers a 1-to-2.5 spend-to-sales ratio.

3. Re-visit SWOT analysis to adjust sales ratio

Now that you determined your sales ratio based on that historical performance, you should re-visit your brand SWOT (recall Step 1 in the Star Brand Model) to see if you need to increase or decrease your ratio depending on other external factors such as distribution challenges, new challengers in the marketplace, etc. You want to adjust your assumptions as needed. Big advertisers for example use various advanced techniques such as mixed market modeling to adjust their assumptions and increase the accuracy of their estimates.

   For simplicity in this Lighting Car example, we do assume the market remains relatively constant versus 2014. After reviewing the competition's behavior over the last few years using Nielsen AdViews, the Lightning Car brand manager felt comfortable assuming that competition would maintain their typical spend levels and media strategy as they have the past three years. Additionally there were no new entrants expected into the category. With this in mind, Lightning Car can move forward with their spend ratio being a direct multiplier (with no further adjustment from market forces) of their money spend through the equation Spend X Spend Ratio = Sales.

4. Calculate your projected spend

With this data, if all things remain constant and the brand's goal is $10 million, then Lightning Car will need to spend $4 million to achieve $10 million in sales in 2015:

2015 Sales Goal = $10,000,000

2014 Spend Ratio = 2.5

Spend X Spend Ratio = Sales

____ X 2.5 = Sales Goal

____X 2.5 = $10,000,000

$4,000,000 X 2.5 = $10,000,000

This Lightning Car exercise is just a simplified budget-setting example intended to show the process behind how historical data points, spend/sales ratio, and market trends can be used to help determine a media budget. Competition, pricing, projected sales, and other factors won't be stagnant, thus you should still adjust your budget assumptions and choices further based on your market realities. There are of course much more complex budget setting approaches using data from statistical models such as Marketing Mix and ROI, SOV and Reach goals. While the process becomes more complicated, with more sophisticated data, the budget will become more accurate as well.

5. Testing your media plan

As you can see, a lot goes into determining the right media plan and the right budget. Thus, the final step in creating a media plan is deciding whether you want to test your media plan or decide to move full force with it in market. While this step is optional, testing your way through a new media plan can be particularly helpful if your brand is in the start up phase (and can't risk a lot of money) or if you need to show results, e.g. market response to the media spending to unlock the marketing funding required for your ideal plan. If your media plan relies on a big news splash, a big reveal, and mass reach, you might need to go full force to truly determine the impact and momentum of all vehicles, versus testing your way through it.

You can scale the test in many ways, based on what you want to learn, for how long and how much you want to spend. For example, you can choose a specific region to test the impact of your media plan. You can also test out with a specific consumer target or prioritize certain vehicles first, i.e. see if digital alone accomplishes your goal.

Starting your media plan in small waves or creating your own media test will allow you to learn on a small scale without much risk and validate the choices you made in your media plans.

A few things to keep in mind as you prepare to test your media plan:

- **Decide test parameters:** What are you trying to learn? Whether the impact of your media budget size, the channels you've chosen, or the consumer you are targeting, clearly understand what you are trying to answer with the test.

- **Identify key performance indicators (KPIs):** What does success mean and how are you going to track it? A test is only of value if you can measure the results. Whether it is awareness lifts or sales, be sure you have a pre-post study in place or a way to measure the impact and can attribute it back to your media plan.

- **Scale:** How big or small do you want your test to be? Clearly define either a region or sub-market that you can isolate and measure the results. Make sure that the test assumptions are representative of your ultimate larger media plan goals, so that if the test is successful, you can easily scale up and expand further.

SUMMARY

Congrats, you just completed Media 101! We reviewed the different market forces that impact the media space, the many media vehicles available, and how to build a media plan and budget.

Brand managers need to craft a robust media strategy, which entails selecting the right budget and media vehicles, in order to get their brand messaging to travel to the right consumers at the right time. Ultimately media, whether it is paid or not, will play a critical role in a achieving a brand's growth goals. Given its importance, we will continue to talk about media, how it fits the brand's overall marketing mix strategy, and its impact throughout the upcoming chapters.

Questions & Review

- How do people become aware of information about brands and products like yours?

- What are the key receptivity insights of your brand target?

- What channels does your target consumer use most?

- Is your brand message more relevant for certain geographies? Certain seasons or events?

- What are the best media vehicles to make your specific brand idea travel effectively?

- What media vehicles have been most effective in driving your type of message in the past?

- What type of media do your lead competitors use? What is their media strategy? How much do they spend?

- What is the brand's spend-to-sales ratio based on your historical data and market analysis?

- What is the media budget needed for your brand to deliver its sales goals?

Establishing the Marketing Strategy

Marketing Strategy & Mix

"Marketing is still an art, and the marketing manager, as head chef, must creatively marshal all his marketing activities to advance the short and long-term interests of his firm."

—Neil H. Borden, 1984

Marketing strategy is the process of creating a plan to deliver the brand's goals of increasing sales and building sustainable brand value. The marketing strategy process requires the previous four steps in the Star Brand Model—brand assessment and goal setting, equity definition, target definition, and the brand's IBI—as well as the marketing mix and a measurement plan that we are about to study.

Given the breadth of components of the marketing strategy and considering that it is a process, we will discuss it across a few chapters, starting from the theory and then moving into putting it into practice. We will begin with an overview of the different components of marketing strategy manifested as the marketing mix. Then we will discuss how to select the right marketing mix to deliver a brand's goal based on what drives effectiveness of each component. With the theory covered, we can go through the steps of building a marketing plan that will turn all the five steps of the Star Brand Model into action to grow your brand. In the last chapter, we will go through how to create a measurement plan to track your brand-building progress and adjust it as needed so you can deliver your ultimate goal. Let's begin.

MARKETING MIX

A core step in developing the marketing strategy for a brand is defining and selecting its marketing mix, which is simply the combination of resources and tactics that can be controlled by a brand to generate sales or build brand awareness. Getting the combination of factors just right, maximizing the return on your investment in getting your product and message out into the world, is one of the biggest challenges a brand manager faces.

The concept of the marketing mix dates back to the late 1940's.[1] Neil H. Borden was the first to use the term, inspired by one of his associates, James Culliton, who described the role of the brand manager as a "mixer of ingredients"; one who sometimes follows recipes prepared by others, sometimes prepares his or her own recipe, sometimes adapts a recipe from immediately available ingredients, and at other times, invents new ingredients no one else has tried.[2] A great analogy for what all great brand managers do well!

Later, classic marketing books described the marketing mix in terms of components, all starting with P, so they could be easily remembered. If you have ever taken a marketing class you will probably know the famous Four Ps—product, price, promotion and place. The Four Ps explain marketing as the activity that puts the right product, at the right place, at the right price, at the right time. Recent marketing books describe the marketing mix with up to Seven Ps—now including components such as people and process.

Let's stay true to the original Four Ps and tie it back to the Star Brand Model that we have been learning. Let's introduce and define the first P: product.

Product

A product is the physical good or the service offered to the customer. Products are the way in which the brand serves a particular consumer need and what consumers buy to solve that need. It is the currency of the brand and consumer relationship. A brand needs to sell products to be called as such.

Traditional thinking will tell you, if you have a good product, it will sell itself. However, in today's highly competitive global market of branded products, there aren't really that many bad products out there anymore. Most of them perform and do what they say on their packaging. Therefore, the real challenge with winning with products today goes beyond performance. Consider how elements such as packaging, a critical experience factor when the consumer first encounters the product, and service, what happens during or after the product usage, can help generate strong consumer preference.

Ask yourself the following questions to better define these characteristics for your product or service:

Performance—how well it functions and satisfies the consumer needs

- What need does the consumer want the product/service to satisfy?
- What features does it have to meet these needs?
- How and where will the consumer use the product?
- How well does it perform vs. competitor products?

Packaging—how attractive is it?

- What does it look like? How will customers experience it?
- What color, size, smell, should it have?
- What is it the product called? How is it branded?
- Does it look better on the shelf than its lead competitor?

Service and Support—what type of after-use warranty or ongoing service it provides

* How will you support the consumer if the product or service doesn't work?
* What types of services are you offering for the consumer to keep using the product/service?
* How does your brand equity and culture support providing great service for your customers?

Having a great product is simply the point of entry if you want to be a Star Brand. If you are a start up, without a great product that consumers love, you might never move past that stage. The overall product experience needs to be differentiated versus the competition. Ideally, the product itself should have great features that uniquely satisfy the consumer's needs; not all consumer needs, but the most important need from the target customer. It should be well branded and have a well-designed package, both aesthetically and ergonomically. Finally, the product or service should offer a way for the consumer to get support in case it fails to meet expectations. Worse than a product not meeting expectations is a poor feedback loop or non-existing customer support. Better yet, service can become a critical point of difference beyond the product and a significant source of brand equity. Think of Zappos, the online shoe and clothing store, for example. Zappos has become one of the world's largest online shoe stores behind a strong culture and focus of delivering "WOW" service to its customers.[3] They go above and beyond, delighting their customers with service in unconventional and innovative ways—surprise VIP account upgrades, 24/7 call center with non-time-constrained customer calls, flowers to show customer appreciation, even helping a customer find a pizza place late at night.

To ensure a brand's product is great, Star Brands invest significant dollars in qualified research and development personnel and product designers and/or experts in user and service design. Having dedicated resources on product design will make products better so that it can be a source of competitive advantage. Strong collaboration between marketing, research, and development and design experts usually yields the best consumer product and service offerings.

Promotion

The promotion elements of the marketing mix capture all the communications and tactics used to encourage consumers to buy a product or service. Without any promotion, the product would be left to sell itself on the shelf, or through word of mouth. To increase sales, you need to promote your product or service. The more you promote your product, the more consumers you will convince of buying it. The most common promotion strategies include advertising and media, price promotion, and sampling.

Advertising and Media

Advertising your product requires a core message persuading potential customers to buy, and then a media investment to broadcast that message. The core brand message stems from your equity pyramid positioning and from the IBI as we studied in previous chapters. The level of media spending, as we learned in media 101, will depend on multiple factors such as the brand's target consumer, the quality and quantity of brand messages as well as the brand's goals, budget, and the competitive landscape.

Price Promotion Incentives

Brands can offer promotional incentives when the cost of the product is a barrier to trial, and can come in many forms and executions. For example, if you want to offer an incentive for a large segment of the population you can insert coupons into the Sunday paper or be part of the deals of major retailers. A discount coupon allows the consumer to buy a product that in theory they wouldn't have bought without the discount incentive.

Other types of price promotions could come in the form of temporary discounts at the store or specific incentives that consumers need to sign up for like points reward cards. This promotion strategy is very common in the retail industry. Big retail events like Memorial Day Weekend sales in the US and Black Friday, which is also now reapplied across markets globally, have become critical volume-driving events for retailers to make their annual numbers. Also, almost every major retail outlet or department store will offer their own credit card with incentives to get customers to return to the store and make additional purchases thanks to the attractive discounts. Next time you buy clothes, pay attention to the person working at the register. He or she will probably offer you a nice discount if you sign up for the credit card or mailing list at the store. That, too, is a promotion strategy.

Frequency of price promotion needs to be well managed, however. If used too frequently, it could potentially impact the perceived brand equity negatively, implying that the product is actually worth less. It could also incent competition to follow heavy price promotion and depress the overall category pricing, thus limiting your ability to keep your pricing strategy long-term.

Sampling

If you have a great product or service experience and your product has a high price, you should have sampling in your marketing mix. Sampling gives the consumer the opportunity to experience the product or service before committing to the purchase and reducing the trial barrier. In the case of consumer goods, samples normally consist of a smaller size package, typically good for one-use size. In the case of cars, it could be a test drive. The sample should be just enough to get the consumer to experience the benefit of the product and decide if it meets her or his needs. The product experience via a sample, if the product is great, should convince the consumer to go and buy it. Sampling is very effective for unique products with obvious and tangible benefits.

Sampling also works well in highly competitive and experiential categories. Think of beauty products. This is an industry where sampling is a core strategy in the marketing mix. There are millions of options available for purchase with new creams, perfumes, and shades of lipsticks introduced practically every week. The amount of beauty products available can be overwhelming to the consumer. However, if a consumer tries a sample of a new product and likes it, they will be more likely to purchase that product in the future. The sample will help reduce the barrier to purchase, especially if the product is high-priced. This is how Sephora and many other beauty stores justify having dedicated personnel to sample their products to virtually any woman who wants to try a product in-store. It helps close the purchase. In the case of services, trial period offers are a very common way to sample. Especially now with the explosion of services online, the best way to get consumers to sign up for a service is to let them use the product for free for a short period of time. This is how Amazon Prime and Netflix are growing their subscription client base.

Sampling can be an experience as well as your total brand proposition. It is very common to find pop-up stores today in major cities that bring the total brand experience to life. Some Star Brands invest in company stores that become a destination for consumers to experience the brand's purpose and the full expression of its visual identity. Nike Town stores in major cities like NYC and Tokyo or the Nivea House in Hamburg, Germany are great examples of sampling taken at a whole different level. Instead of product sampling, corporate stores are brand sampling. They help built affinity for the brands among the people that love them and at a minimum it drives brand awareness among tourists in major cities and potential customers.

Placement

Placement, in the context of a marketing mix, represents the physical or virtual place where the product or service can be purchased. This is commonly referred to as the distribution channel. The ideal distribution channel for a brand is one that makes the product available to the consumer at the right place, the right time, and in the right quantities.

Consumers shop in all kinds of places: family stores, specialty stores, department stores, mass merchandisers, malls, outdoors markets, and online. In order to determine the right place for the brand to be distributed, the brand manager needs to understand where the target consumer shops and is most likely to look for the specific product category. The shopping pattern for your particular product might be unique as well. The point of sale for the product should be intuitive for the consumer in terms of the types of product that the retail outlet normally carries and the positioning of your brand—high end, value brand, specialized, etc. Is the product being available at selective distribution channels critical to your brand positioning? Or is being available in as many high frequency outlets as possible more important? If you are a luxury brand or highly specialized product, consumers aren't likely to look for you at mass merchandisers like Walmart or dollar stores where consumers go for low prices. Instead, for a luxury brand you should achieve selective distribution at high-end department stores like Neiman Marcus or specialty stores where your target consumer is more likely to shop.

The right timing and right quantities in which your product is offered can also help decide the type of distribution channels that would provide the best shopping experience. For example, e-commerce is redefining the concept of shopping ease and immediacy and providing a wider availability of options. Online retailers like Amazon, with services such as Prime Pantry and Dash, deliver household products in less than two days with low, flat-cost shipping. Their Dash device allows customers to shop for items away from their computer by simply scanning bar codes in their kitchen, to easily replenish items. Services like these, among others, have the potential to reinvent distribution channels and dramatically improve the shopping experience in the future.

Price

Price is the amount a consumer pays for the product or service the brand offers. Pricing includes the list price of the actual product and also any financing and other payment options that the consumer uses to acquire it.

Pricing is the marketing mix variable that can have the largest impact on your brand financials and profit. As such, pricing decisions should take into account the profit margins you expect to deliver as a brand. After all, the price that you set is what determines how much money there is left to spend in marketing once you cover all the expenses needed to produce the product and put it into the consumer's hands. The price for the product or service has to be right for the consumer, so it is appealing to buy, and right for the brand, so it makes a profit.

The price strategy you set for the product is also a critical component of the brand proposition as it sends a strong signal to the consumer about the positioning and the quality of the product. Consumers typically equate low prices to poor quality products while higher prices signal uniqueness and high quality. Also, the price difference versus the lead competitor can signal how differentiated the product is and potentially its superiority. The frequency of promotion can also affect the brand's value perception.

The right price for the product is the one that accurately captures the perceived value of the benefit the product provides to the consumer. If the price is too high for the perceived benefit, the consumer will determine this is poor value and won't buy the product. Consumers will compare your price versus the next available product option on shelf. Your pricing should reflect the perceived value the consumer is receiving and be as attractive as the next lead competitor in your competitive set.

In sum, when setting the price for the product, in addition to considering whether it makes sense financially—that is, your overall pricing strategy—consider the signal the pricing will give the consumer regarding the quality of the product based on the price difference you are setting versus lead competitive products..

SUMMARY

Understanding in depth the different components of marketing mix, Product, Promotion, Placement and Price, you are well on your way to establish a marketing strategy for your brand. Let's now learn in the next chapter about the brand math formula and how it can help you select the right marketing mix to achieve your specific brand goals.

Selecting the Marketing Mix

"When you can measure what you are talking about and express it in numbers, you know something about it."

— Lord William Thomson Kelvin, British mathematical physicist
   and engineer (1824-1907)

We just reviewed the different components of the marketing mix. All of them can play a distinct role in driving sales. Now, how do you select the right mix of components to deliver a specific brand goal? How will the components work best together? To answer these questions we will reach out for what we learned in eighth grade. Algebra! Yes, the best way to map out how the marketing mix delivers actual brand sales is in terms of a mathematical formula. I call it the brand math formula. Mastering this concept will help you select the right marketing mix and help you forecast how you will get to your brand goal. But before we get to the brand math formula, let's understand first how brand sales are generated.

BRAND SALES: TRIAL AND REPEAT

Brand sales are a result of consumers buying your product for the first time, also called brand trial, and repeating a purchase of your brand over their lifetime, brand repeat. The rate in which they buy or use the product or service over time will also impact the quantity of the brand's sales. The higher percentage of people in the population who are trying and repeating a purchase and the more often they do it, the more volume the brand sells.

Here is how the cycle of generating trial and repeat works. First, in order to generate brand trial and repeat you need to have an attractive proposition consumers are aware of and can physically find in the market to buy. But before people can consider buying a product, they need to first become aware of the brand. The brand message should be persuasive and reach the customer when he or she is most receptive to it. Then when the consumer goes to the store to look for it or browse online they need to be able to find it to purchase it. The product should be available in the right sizes or service terms to meet the need of the consumer usage habit. If the consumer has a positive experience he or she is likely to come back for a second purchase. All brands want the same thing: more consumers buying its products and for them to become loyal.

A strong marketing mix is one that delivers the following:

* Effective marketing investment that makes people aware and persuaded to buy
* Appealing product/service proposition with good value and usage experience
* Availability of the product for purchase at the right places and right quantities

BRAND MATH FORMULA

The brand math formula provides an easy mathematical format to explain the impact a particular marketing mix has on brand sales. The formula helps you understand how each variable contributes to driving brand sales, allowing you to optimize further and select the best marketing mix. You can also use it to forecast future sales at a high level based on the different marketing mix inputs. The ideal marketing mix for a brand will be the one that maximizes the brand's math formula volume, i.e. brand sales.

Brand Sales = Awareness x Appeal x Distribution x Usage

Let's break the formula down by its components. First, the output of the formula will be the sales of your product or service that can be measured in any tangible metric in which your transaction takes place. It can be any other currency your brand operates in or the actual units used for the transaction. For example if you are a spirit brand your units can be bottles or if you are Direct TV it could be number of subscribers.

Second, the operands or variables of the brand math formula—awareness, appeal, distribution, and usage—capture the impact of the selected marketing mix, recall these are brand choices across product, price, promotion, and placement. These variables will directly influence the volume and number of sales of your service or product. Depending on how these variables perform, the more or less volume output you will get in brand sales. The bigger and more positive each of the operands are the more sales the brand will achieve.

Let's now study each variable in detail. To illustrate further how the different marketing mix components impact these variables, some will have additional mathematical formulas within.

Brand Awareness

% of population aware of your brand = media spending X quality of message

Awareness as a variable captures the impact of marketing mix strategies in promotion such as advertising, media, and also placement to some degree. Brand awareness is the number of people in the national population that know the brand exists and what it stands for. If consumers don't know the brand exists they can't buy it. The more people are aware of a brand, the more people are likely to buy it. This is why large brands will typically invest significant amount of dollars in mass reach vehicles like TV to increase the number of people aware of the brand and increasing the likelihood of the brand being in the consumers' consideration set.

Brand awareness is a direct output of brand exposure, which can be achieved via media spending, other people talking about your brand (e.g. earned media either via free publicity or word of mouth) or wide availability of the product. Since we will cover availability when we discuss distribution, let's focus primarily on the promotion drivers of awareness.

Awareness will be the most direct output metric of a brand's media spending. The level of media spending and the types of vehicles chosen will affect the effectiveness of the media investment. For the advertising message to be effec-

tive, it should reach consumers when they are most receptive: when your category is relevant or the message is appropriate to the media vehicle.

Awareness of the brand will also be impacted by the quality of the message. Is the message clear and consistent? Can consumers recall the brand? If there is too much noise and inconsistency of what a brand stands for, it becomes harder for the consumer to remember it. Also the quality of the message, which is the ability of the idea to persuade to buy and promote the brand, will impact how many people have a good quality awareness of your brand.

The quality of your message ultimately depends on the ability of the advertised

Coca-Cola remains one of the world's most ubiquitous brands.

message to persuade the consumers to buy. A high quality messaging is one that makes consumers aware of a brand's benefits and converts them into actual buyers. Here is where the quality of the idea can really contribute to creating more effective awareness of your brand.

Appeal

Product Value = Benefit / Price

This variable captures the impact from the marketing mix strategy on product, pricing, and promotion. Brand appeal is how attractive the product or service you offer is for people to buy. Appeal for the consumer will be derived from how well the consumer perceives the product to satisfy their needs and preferences versus other product choices. The higher the appeal, the higher the likelihood that the product will be preferred among many choices. There are different product offerings that can satisfy one particular need. To select the right one, the consumer evaluates the options available based on how well they can satisfy the particular need that drives their purchase interest and its perceived value. The value of a particular product or service proposition is determined by how attractive the benefit is that the product provides, weighted by the price the consumer needs to pay to acquire it. In general, consumers will be seeking to get the most value for their money.

The ultimate value of the proposition is how much money the consumer is willing to give up in exchange for acquiring the product or service. The more attractive the product, the more the consumer is willing to pay. However, if the product cost outweighs the benefit the product provides in the consumer's mind, the less appealing it is and thus the consumer is less likely to buy it. Brands need to offer attractive product benefits at the right price. Let's look at both components of the product appeal value equation, benefit, and price.

Let's talk first about the role the benefit has on the product appeal and its perceived value. Products that are unique and have strong performance attributes superior to other competitive products are more appealing to consumers than average products. They provide a greater perceived benefit. The benefit of the product is communicated to the consumer across all the different brand touch points, the product itself and the brand communication being the primary ones. The more persuasive the communication on the pack or in advertising, the more likely the consumer will be compelled to buy a product for the first time. Once a consumer purchases the product or service, how well the product meets the consumer's expectation will determine if the consumer will buy the product again or not. A positive product usage experience is what makes a repeat purchase possible. If the product or service meets or exceeds the expectation created at the first purchase, the consumer is likely to repeat the product purchase in the future. If the product experience is poor, the consumer won't likely buy the product again. For a product or service proposition to last over time in market, it needs to be designed so that it is attractive to buy but also that it delivers its promised performance so that the consumer can continue to buy it over their lifetime. It is really difficult to build a brand only on a trial or one-time use. You need the consumer who buys your product and comes back for more.

Now let's talk about price as the denominator of the value equation that also affects the product appeal. Pricing should be set to suggest the ideal value for the consumer given the benefit being offered. If the pricing of the product changes, the perceived value for the consumer will change as well. For certain categories, increasing prices could be devastating to the volume sales, especially if competition doesn't raise prices along. This is because there is a poorer perceived value to the consumer compared with other choices available for purchase. However, if the volume drop that comes from a price increase is less than the profit gained, it could still be a good financial strategy for the brand if the main priority is to deliver on financial expectations. If the cost of goods increases dramatically, manufacturers are often forced to increase prices to keep their financial profile whole. Conversely, lowering the price of a product could improve sales volume positively. However, it can severely impact the brand's ability to deliver its profit that year. This is why lowering prices is typically only used if you are in a defensive growth strategy.

Promotion incentives can also increase the appeal of the product or service offering. These incentives reduce the price, thus the value of the products will improve in the eyes of the consumer. However, these incentives should only be temporary tactics to use around new product introductions or seasonal promotions. The appeal of the product or service shouldn't be highly dependent on these incentives for consumers to buy it.

Incentives like sales promotions and samples can enhance the appeal of the product proposition as they will either reduce the need for cash outlay or reduce the perceived risk by experiencing the product first. These are important marketing mix investment choices to promote trial of a product, which is particularly important if the product is new to market.

Distribution

Distribution = number of outlets carrying the brand / total number of outlets

Distribution captures the impact of the marketing mix's placement strategy. It refers to the availability of the product for the consumer, and how it is distributed has a direct correlation to the brands sales. Once a consumer is aware, he or she will need to be able to find the product to be able to buy it. Often, the first time a consumer will become aware of the product will be the point of sale. Therefore, distribution influences awareness positively. Depending of the model for your brand, distribution is typically measured as the number of retailer points where your brand is sold. This can be measured in number of stores and retailers. In the case of services, it can be measured by the number of outlets where the services are offered or number of sales representatives reaching consumers. For many businesses, distribution will be the number one business driver so significant effort will be placed in building relationships with retailers or building platforms like e-commerce portal to make the product available to consumers.

Distribution has typically a linear correlation with sales volume. Therefore, the broader you go in distribution outlets the more volume your will achieve. This is why it is common for a brand to expand into multiple retail channels: small retail, large retail, and online, for example. But also as distribution grows across channels, the productivity per point of distribution might decline. Therefore the brand manager and the sales team need to be careful to expand distribution only at the rate that sales productivity can be maintained with each incremental sales location. However, in my experience you should welcome and celebrate any time you gain new distribution for your brand, provided it is a place where the consumer can find the product. Better to be available to more consumers than less if you want to build a brand further.

90% of all Americans live within 15 miles of a Walmart store, making them an attractive distribution channel.

When a product is distributed in new places, it reaches more potential customers. When small brands are able to gain distribution in retail chains with mass reach like Walmart or Target or Best Buy for technology, they are no longer small brands. For consumer goods brands there is clearly a life before and after being successful at Walmart, the largest retail chain in America with two hundred million visitors per week. The moment distribution of the product increases, so will its sales. Often the steepest sales growth happens thanks to new distribution; therefore it is a critical marketing mix variable to influence and track.

Usage

Volume per customer = volume size per purchase X frequency of purchase

Usage as a variable captures the impact of marketing mix strategies of product and pricing. Usage refers to the quantities and frequency in which your brand is being purchased on average. Changes to transaction size and frequency of purchase will have an impact on your sales volume equation.

Volume per customer is a measure that captures how often a consumer will buy a product and in which quantities. This variable will directly affect the brand sales, especially over an extended period of time. If the consumer uses more of your product, the transaction size is likely to be larger or the frequency of purchase higher.

The purchase cycle of your product and the transaction size in which it is offered will directly affect the brand's volume quantity. The package sizes in which you offer your product should be designed to meet the consumers' expectations in length of usage but also in price per use. Often consumers expect larger sizes to offer better value than smaller packaging.

The product should be designed in a way that it delivers on the recommended usage and drives your desired sales volume. Talking to potential customers can help you understand the ideal size they would want to acquire based on the intended use. Also, there could be important price points associated with the number of usage or perhaps the length of the service provided. For example, global brands will make available larger size products in developed countries where club stores or mass merchandisers are more prevalent. In developing countries where more consumers have less cash outlay, smaller stores are more prevalent and so are smaller product sizes. Think of shampoo for example. In the United States a significant part of the shampoo sales are done in larger sizes. In India, the sales of a one- to two-use shampoo sachets are a bigger portion of the category sales. This also applies to services. In developed countries, cable is mostly purchased via one-year subscriptions. In some countries in Latin America it can be purchased by day or month given the cash outlay considerations.

Pricing and sizing can also be manipulated to generate more usage to impact sales. For example, smaller sizes of a product at lower price points or value size packages can motivate the consumer to buy the product if they haven't purchased it in the past, or make an incremental purchase that will likely trigger more product use. You can also impact transaction size even if the product is in market already via promotional tactics. For example Buy 1, Get 1 or combo packs (two products bundled together) offers are common tactics to drive more volume for the brand and hopefully more consumption.

Overall, changes to transaction size and frequency of purchase can have a large impact in your sales volume equation. Given their importance, ideally they should be built into the product design, and if not, later influenced promotionally once in market.

SUMMARY

You have conquered the theory in Step 4: Establishing the Marketing Strategy! By understanding what each marketing mix component can do to impact a brand's goal and how to mix the right components for your brand's marketing strategy, you are now ready to build a marketing plan in the final step of the Star Brand Model.

Questions & Review

- What are the most critical components of your marketing mix? Are some more important than others?
- What are your product's trial barriers? Which elements of the marketing mix can help address them?
- How many people need to try your product to meet your brand goals?
- How many consumers do you need to repeat a purchase?
- How many people need to be aware of your product to meet your brand goals?
- How appealing is your current product proposition? How unique is your benefit?
- How does its perceived value compare versus a leading competitive product?
- What is the ideal price for your product? What is the price difference versus other competitive products?
- How likely is a consumer to buy your product once they have sampled it?
- How much does your brand rely on price promotion? How does competition promote their products?
- Where and in how many points of distribution does your product need to be sold at to meet your brand goals?
- How frequently and in which sizes do you need consumers to buy your product to meet your brand goals? Is there a desired consumer size for your offering?
- Are you impacting the right variables of the Brand Math formula sufficiently? How likely are you to reach your brand goals?

Building the Marketing Plan & Measurement

The
Marketing Plan

"A goal without a plan is just a wish."

– Antoine de Saint-Exupéry

The marketing strategy for a brand can be developed for multiple years; however, the strategy becomes really tangible when written in a plain format with a specific time frame of execution. That is the objective of the marketing plan. The marketing plan is the key document to express what is needed to accomplish the brand's goals for a specific time frame, most often a year. In this document the brand manager outlines the overall marketing strategies, priorities, resources and key activities to be executed to deliver the brand's goals on a specific timeframe. The marketing plan becomes the executional blueprint of the brand's marketing strategy.

The five steps in the Star Brand Model have helped you make key strategic choices for your brand that will help set its trajectory. If you've already made a set of choices for how the brand will show up in market, you might argue, "Why can't I just go and do them?" Why do you need really need a marketing plan? Here is the reality of managing a brand. Having a brilliant strategy without a plan to execute won't get you far. Not having a strategy is a non-starter, for sure. Once you have a strategy, you need to turn that into an operational plan that can be carried out by the entire team to make it a reality. Otherwise, strategy is just a paper exercise. You need to execute the strategy brilliantly for it to have any value.

Consider each of the theoretical elements we discussed in the five steps as building blocks of the brand's marketing strategy that will become a section of the marketing plan document. This approach will allow you to easily build a marketing plan on your own. The marketing plan will give structure to the brand analysis, vision setting, equity, target, and idea definition that you have completed. The marketing plan will turn the brand strategy choices into tactical activities to execute in market. Here are some additional benefits you should expect from having a marketing plan for your brand.

The marketing plan will help allocate the right resources to the right activities. In any company, even if it is successful and booming, resources are limited. Every day investors face many pressures of where to allocate money, resources, or time, from simply covering the basics like payroll and the cost of operations to future investments like building a plant or acquiring another brand. So in one way or another other, resources in any company are precious and up for grabs by different competing priorities. In the case of brands, if the company is mid- to large-size, investment needs to be prioritized among a portfolio of other brands or/and other investments. More often than not, the authority over these resources lies at a very high level of the organization and not with the brand manager. Thus, one of the most difficult tasks a brand manager will face is getting management to buy into the plan he or she wants to execute. To do so, the brand manager needs to prove he or she has a solid plan that balances the time, money, and resources needed to accomplish their ultimate business goal. Management will be evaluating how well a marketing plan will yield the return on investment and whether it is realistic and worth prioritizing over other funding choices.

The marketing plan will be the ultimate "showcase" of the brand's marketing strategy. In the marketing plan the brand manager is expected to showcase the future vision for the brand, the results that are possible to achieve, and the plan to deliver them. It's a comprehensive document. It gives the opportunity to the brand manager to lead the brand's thinking and influence management to get the resources needed to be effective at the job. If the marketing plan is compelling and includes exciting plans, the brand manager will also build trust and hope in management. Ultimately, the brand managers' results, which are the brand results, will be management's results too. If the brand manager doesn't present a compelling marketing plan, he or she won't get the resources needed to carry out their vision for the brand. The resources will go somewhere else to fund another brand or a more compelling plan in a different department. Getting the marketing plan approved by management is a vote of confidence in the brand manager's vision and the reward is that he or she secures the resources needed to carry out the plan.

Finally, building a marketing plan will be a calibration process for the complete brand and multi-functional team. Through each discussion on the set of choices to be made to build the brand, the plans will hopefully become clearer and better. So it is during the process of creating the marketing plan that the magic happens. The brand manager is both the leader and moderator of the marketing process and it is his or her responsibility to tap into the best thinking of all the team resources and agencies throughout. A strong brand manager leading the team through the process knows when the team needs to diverge into more free-flow thinking to come up with more ideas and when to converge to land these ideas with defined scope and numbers. The process of building both the marketing plan and the document will serve as a map to guide all functions to reach the ultimate brand objective and assign tasks based on the expertise needed.

The marketing plan is both a document and a process to solidify the brand's marketing strategy and the plans to follow and execute against. Next we will discuss the structure of the marketing plan and how to populate it based on what you have learned in all the previous chapters.

MARKETING PLAN TIMELINE

Brand growth expectations are typically set and refreshed every year, as there will be new expectations, challenges, and ideas that require planning and allocation of resources. Therefore, brands typically go through an annual planning process to set out the business and brand goals and strategies for the upcoming year. The most common time frame for marketing plans is one year, but they can vary from company to company, brand to brand, or industry to industry, and they are typically closely aligned with the company's financial cycle. Regardless of the fiscal year of the brand, the brand team needs to begin to develop their marketing plans for the following year at least six months prior. In the case of big new product or service launches, marketing plan preparation could begin twelve to eighteen months in advance.

THE STRUCTURE OF A MARKETING PLAN

The marketing plan document needs to be as comprehensive as possible and tailored to the audience, whether it is for approval of the decision maker, a management team, or the brand team. The overall content should tell the story of what the brand wants to accomplish, the plan to accomplish it, and the key indicators of success. The marketing plan serves as a business proposal and once approved the plan becomes a commitment to action.

Since the marketing plan is a physical document it is helpful to explain its components and how to build one using the order in which the information should be presented. Depending on the organization's preference in written communication, whether it is a one-page document or PowerPoint slides, the look and feel of the marketing plan will vary across companies. Also, if the culture is more informal there might be less rigor in the level of detail included. Regardless of the preferred style, the marketing plan should be handled and communicated as a business proposal that outlines how a specific business objective can be achieved with a set of strategy and investment choices for the brand. Also, it should be presented to the stakeholders who can approve and unleash the funding to begin the market activation of the plan if approved.

In any business endeavor where you are trying to sell an idea, you need to build a compelling story that gets the audience excited and convinces them to invest. The more appealing the idea, the more solid your arguments, and the less perceived risk there is for the investor, the more likely you will gather investors for your idea. The marketing plan is no different. You need to convince your management or whoever holds access to the funds that your plan will give the results promised.

I will now explain how to present the different marketing strategy components in a formal marketing plan. I will present them in the order in which they help build the story for your marketing plan proposal.

Executive Summary

The marketing plan starts with a clear statement of purpose—the ultimate business objective—which is the basis for the consideration of any business proposal. Therefore, a marketing plan should start with a brief articulation of the current brand status and then move on to describing the vision and goal that the plan seeks to achieve. It should also include what the document seeks to accomplish, in most cases approval for funding and execution of the marketing plan.
This will serve as the executive summary of the document.

Background

To establish the context, use the internal and market analysis from Step 1 of the Star Brand Model. The summary of that exercise serves as the brand context to describe the brand's current status and its challenges. That is where you are starting from. It should include your assessment of the key strengths and opportunities that should be leveraged and the key weaknesses and threats that need to be addressed. The background should read like a story, serving as a rationale for the marketing strategy you are recommending.

Vision

After the context, indicate the overall vision of where you want the brand to go—basically, the desired brand growth trajectory. Recall from the vision exercises in Chapter 3, the articulation of the vision should be simple, inspiring, stretching, and capture the brand's uniqueness and strategic intent.

Goals and Objectives

To support the vision, clearly state the specific brand objectives and goals for the year you are building the marketing plan for. The goal should be bold but achievable, grounded on the realities of the brand. The brand goal should be articulated with performance metrics like sales, market share, and profit. Consider including in this section charts with numbers to better illustrate what you are going after.

Depending on where the brand stands in its development cycle, the marketing plan should articulate what type of business strategy the team is pursuing for the upcoming year. These selected metrics will signal the type of business strategy the brand is after. It is important to state what the next year is supposed to do in terms of the brand trajectory. Is the objective to grow the brand significantly or just maintain current performance? Will you focus on defending your current market position if there is a major competitive threat? Or is the brand in such a state that it is best to harvest it in the short term and stop investing in its future? Be clear on the strategy intent and of course be as detailed as possible as to how that strategy looks.

Use all the brand and market analysis conducted to articulate your specific strategy. If it is a growth strategy, perhaps you need to focus on making a new product as successful as possible to unleash new sales. If it is a sustaining strategy, add specificity when listing the core elements from the previous year's strategy and execution that you should absolutely maintain. If you need to protect and defend the brand due to changes in competitive environment, will you do that with pricing or innovation? Determine how you will compete in market. Finally, if you are milking the brand, state the few things that you will still do to deliver the profit. Set up goals that clearly signal your strategy, what you will and will not do.

Marketing Strategy

The core of the marketing plan is your recommendation of how the brand can achieve the brand goals for the particular year with a proposed marketing strategy.

For this section you will use Steps 2 to 4 of the Star Brand Model, which include the brand equity positioning, the brand's target, and your selected marketing mix.

Here is how the different components of the marketing strategy can be fleshed out in a marketing plan document and become rationale points to build confidence in your plan and secure the funding you are requesting.

Equity

The brand equity positioning is simply stated on the document to remind the audience what the brand stands for and the basis for brand communication. You can include the brand ideal and brand promise as the core elements of your positioning (recall this is the tip of the Pyramid). The full equity pyramid can be part of the appendix.

Target

Describe your brand's target. This should include your needs segment as well as any particular sub-segment that you consider important to reach with this marketing plan in the short term. The target consumer that you list should be the main target of the brand's communication proposed for that year. Include the key insights you have about your target and if available the key trial barriers that you are trying to overcome. The information that you include about the target will give meaning to the marketing plan tactics you propose. Ultimately the consumer is the audience for all brand-marketing activities. Include only the information that is most actionable. For example, core needs, brand perceptions, insights, barriers to trial, media receptivity, and a description of what matters to your target customer. You can include detailed information about your target consumer, like a detailed consumer profile in the appendix as well. You can also bring your consumer to life the day of your marketing plan presentation if you think this would work well with the audience that is approving your plan.

Marketing Mix

The marketing mix includes the specific market choices in your plan such as product, promotion—e.g., advertising and media, price promotion, etc.—pricing, and distribution. The multi-functional team building the marketing mix plan will need to put a stake in the ground for each of these elements and demonstrate how each contributes to building the desired sales.

Product

Describe the characteristics of the product offering that you will focus your marketing efforts on. If it is a new product or service, include its unique benefits, consumer appeal, and expected sales that support launching it. If there is any consumer data on the appeal of the product include it as rationale. Also call out the hero products or variants that you are planning on featuring in your marketing activations to emphasize focus.

Communication: Advertising & Media

Since a brand can develop multiple ideas to advertise different products, the marketing plan needs to spell out exactly which lead idea (or ideas in the case of multiple products), you are recommending to launch as the main message that will compel consumers to buy. All you need to do is reflect the articulation of the idea and if available highlight why you believe the idea drives brand or product appeal and relevance among the target consumer. If you did research with consumers on it, highlight what you learned. Use any data or sound bites that hint at the idea's ability to break through the clutter. Ideas that have high appeal, drive recall of your brand, and are persuasive will make your marketing more effective and garner more sales.

Media-wise, list the key vehicles that you chose to communicate the message. You can justify them based on consumer receptivity insights or previous ROI data or historical results. It is common to prioritize the vehicles in order of importance and include the estimated percentage of each to the total media spend and anticipated reach or impressions. You can easily show this on a chart.

Other Promotions

It is common to use other promotional tactics such as consumer purchase incentives—coupons, anniversary sales, gift sets, sampling, or custom brand experiences. If they are important to persuade the particular target you are going after, include them in the plan with some rationale and the approximate spend you are putting them against. It is also helpful to show how these other promotional tactics will work in tandem with your communications plan.

Pricing

If critical to your strategy, clearly state your brand's pricing strategy for the upcoming year. This is particularly important if you are making pricing changes like taking prices up or down. If that is the case, list the specific expectations coming from that tactic and how you are planning to implement it. If you are focusing on promotional pricing tactics, include the type of pricing promotions or incentives you plan on offering and chart them ideally on a timetable of when they will be available for the consumer.

Distribution

Articulate what success looks like in terms of your distribution channels that include key channels or retailers you will focus on. If your stated brand goals and strategy depend on achieving increased distribution, explain how you intend to achieve it including incentives, associated costs, and any product priorities. Explain what products you are in most need of to get to the right place and the right time and which channels you will use to accomplish it.

Marketing Budget

The marketing spending that you are proposing needs to be consistent with the sales, market share, and profit goals you are promising in the top section of the document. Include an overall budget for all your marketing expenditures as well as a detailed media budget, likely the largest portion of your spend.

To justify your choices, reference how this investment relates to historical spending or versus benchmarks from competition or similar categories. Also, prioritize the spending by marketing mix element based on the level of impact each will have in generating sales and also the level of spending. Create a priority list of your marketing spending so it is clear which buckets you would fund first or re-prioritize if you don't get the full budget amount you are requesting. Finally, since there are many ways to arrive at a media and marketing budget, I suggest you share your specific analysis and assumptions in the appendix of the marketing plan.

Measurement, Risks, and Contingency Plan

To build confidence with the marketing plan audience, you should call out how you plan to measure progress, any known risks, and any contingency efforts you will set if problems arise. Having a solid measurement plan will give management confidence that you have put in place a disciplined approach to track performance and are able to adjust plans accordingly. This section serves as the risk management perspective of the marketing plan. In the next chapter, we will go in depth on how to build a detailed measurement plan, how to select the core metrics, how you break them down by traceable periods and the key action steps that you will take based on their performance. The measurement and performance plan will be the key tool to use continuously to determine if your marketing plan is on track.

NEXT STEPS

A marketing plan is a document that drives action. As such it should have clear expectation on the next steps following the review of the plan. These should include when final approval is expected, dates and gates for funding requirements, and the most critical upcoming dates to implement the plan. You can also assign specific owners of each of the next steps to drive additional accountability. Make sure that before you wrap up a marketing plan meeting you end with an agreement on specific next steps.

To give you an idea of what a marketing plan might look like following the format we just discussed, here is an example of a marketing plan I created for US Harley Davidson for their upcoming marketing planning cycle in 2015. The document provides in one page a thorough overview of the brand's situation, the vision and objectives for the following year, the marketing strategy along with the marketing mix and budget, and finally the measurement and contingency plan. Marketing plans tend to be longer than one page or a comprehensive PowerPoint presentation with much more detailed information in

Harley Davidson US 2015
MARKETING PLAN RECOMMENDATION

This recommends $20MM marketing plan to grow US Harley Davidson
by 10% in 2015 outreaching to a younger "Freedom rider" target.

Background

In 2014 Harley Davidson (HD) grew sales in the US by 5% and sustained market share behind increased sales among its existing customer base "Freedom Riders 35+". HD still leads the +601cc bike category segment and its equity remains strong. However, share gap versus competition is narrowing as the lead competitor is making strides with younger consumers (bike purchases among 35< is 160 IYA vs. 35+ 110 IYA). This market dynamic threatens HD's ability to sustain long-term growth. To deliver its long-term growth objective, HD needs to step change its growth rate to at least 10% driving relevance among a younger customer base.

Vision & 2015 Business Objectives

HD's long-term vision is to move from being a well-known American motorcycle brand relevant to an older generation to become a more relevant brand that unleashes people's dreams of personal freedom. To deliver this vision long term, in 2015 we are looking to advance category leadership (+5 points) and deliver a 10% increase in sales and profit.

	2014 Sales (IYA)	2015 Sales Reco (IYA)
Volume (Units)	50,000 (102)	55,000 (110)
Non- Entry level Bike Units	40,000	42, 000 (105)
Entry Level Bike Units	10,000	13,000 (130)
Sales ($MM)	$100MM (105)	$ 110MM(110)
Marketing Spending ($MM)	$18 (105)	$20 (111)
Market Share (%)	40.0	45% (+5 points)
Profit	$35MM	$38.50MM (110)

Note: All bikes currently deliver the same margin. IYA: Index vs Year Ago

Marketing Plan Recommendation

To achieve a 10% increase in sales in 2015 we recommend a total marketing spending of $20MM (111 IYA). This plan is slightly higher than historical spending (+$2MM) in order to effectively outreach a new younger sub-segment with our entry-level bike. The proposed plan will expand our customer base to sure up HD's long-term growth and share leadership.

2015		Marketing Budget								
Estimates		Sub-Totals						Total	
Volume (units)	Market Share	Media	PR	HOG	Prom	Adv. Production	Digital Promo	Dollars	Marketing $/Bike
55,000	45%	$8.5MM	$5.5MM	$2.5MM	$1.0MM	$1.5MM	$1.0MM	$20MM	$362

Note: Average Bike retail price $20M

Sample "One Page" Marketing Plan - front.

Marketing Mix Rationale

Drive awareness and trial among the growing younger sub-segment of "Freedom Riders" by positioning HD in a more relevant way. Market research indicates that to drive awareness and relevance among the new sub-segment, who is more likely to be multi-cultural and digitally savvy (See consumer profile in appendix), HD needs to reach them across multiple relevant touch-points (Online/ER). New HD trial will be driven by overcoming our biggest trial barrier ("HD is not relevant for me, I am not that old") with more relevant communication and media vehicles. The media increase (111 IYA) is needed to achieve discontinuous awareness among this target.

Win with entry-level bike HD Street 500cc/ 700cc to allure younger sub-segment. HD's entry-level bikes have a more modern look and feel and are better designed to meet the needs of the younger first time HD buyers. While these bikes are currently distributed in all dealerships, they are not heavily promoted. Plan is to heavily feature them in promotional tools that reach the younger target i) Digital offers ii) PR and Earned media opportunities iii) Targeted HOG efforts iv) New Digital Catalogue.

Activate Loyal "Freedom riders 35+" as brand ambassadors with sustaining HOG support. Market research indicates that loyal riders are open to buying additional products from HD and are very likely to recommend the brand to others. Focus will be on creating new experiences for the TOP HOGs and for them to invite new members to join the HD family. Focus will be the non-entry level bikes.

Based on the above rationale, the cascading marketing priorities for the brand are listed:

Marketing Mix Element	Cost ($MM)	Rank	IYA	Notes
Digital	$5.5	1	108	New communication idea for younger sub-segment featuring entry level bikeHolistic online/ off-line integration; Generate viral/ aid conversion via website, display and video ads, social media, OOH ad placement in relevant locations, etc.
Out of Home	$1.5			
Total Media	$8.5			
Public Relations + Earned media	$5.5	2	105	Relevant events in places where and when the sub- segment is receptive. WOM/buzz (short-lead e.g. blogs, Pop culture influencers, music festivals, racing activities)
HOG Marketing	$2.5	3	100	Breakthrough Experiences for loyalists with built-in opportunities to become ambassadors.
Digital Promotion	$1.0	4	N/A	Digital promotion 2X a year to promote entry level bike e.g. Test Drive Rider's Edge Academy
Advertising Production	$1.5	N/A	102	Agency and advertising production cost, increase consistent with additional creative executions
Total	$20		108	

Note: IYA: Index vs Year Ago

Measurement and Contingency Plan

We will report progress monthly across business performance, consumer and marketing effectiveness metrics. Our biggest risk it not being able to capture the younger consumer as effectively as the competition. Our measurement plan will include a detailed contingency plan.

Next Steps

Approval to plan by August 30, 2014
Marketing Executions Produced by December 2014
Plan Release Jan 1st, 2015

Note: Hypothetical Marketing plan created by Author 1,2. Not real HD figures.

Sample "One Page" Marketing Plan -back

the appendices such as media plans, financial forecast, product specifications, etc. However, I want to point out that what matters most, your clear brand strategy and solid thinking, should be able to fit in one page. This will allow your marketing plan to be a quick study in case your audience has limited time and also becomes an ongoing, one-stop-shop reference document.[4,5]

Presenting the Marketing Plan

Once you have built your marketing plan document, prepare to have a powerful presentation. Your objective should be getting the approval of the strategy and more importantly the resources that you need to set it in motion. Hopefully you already understand the approver audience well and know which key areas would be most interesting to them regarding how you plan to deliver the goals that you are promising. Cater your presentation to the timing and format that your audience is most comfortable with. Don't turn the marketing plan document into a long PowerPoint deck if your time with Management is short. I once heard that you shouldn't send a PowerPoint to do a document's job. Also, think of potentially sending pre-reading materials in advance. Any documents that you present should be clear and deliver on their intent: propose a brand-building plan and secure the resources to carry it forward.

Assuming you are successful, once you have the approval for the plan, the next thing to do is communicate the final marketing plans to the broader organization and begin implementation. Make sure all the key players on your team, especially those that will execute it, understand the plan clearly.

SUMMARY

You have learned how to put together a marketing plan for your brand! This is the culmination of the Star Brand Model in a tangible plan that you can act against to build, market, and manage your brand. Once you have the green light to execute the marketing plan, it is just a matter of putting all the right brand manager skills into practice and having the operational discipline and executional leadership to lead the team to achieve the marketing plan goals that were promised. To ensure you stay on track, you should build a measurement plan. We will learn how to do that next, in our last chapter and final step of the Star Brand Model.

Measurement Plan

The final step in developing a marketing strategy is to create a plan to monitor progress in market and set contingency efforts if problems arise. A brand's measurement plan helps track how your plan is performing versus the ultimate goal and provides diagnostic measures of your likelihood of success. The measurement plan defines how success will be measured and how risks associated with the proposed brand-building plan will be managed.

Brand managers are expected to go deep into understanding what the metrics in a measurement plan say about the marketing strategy put in place, and to build intervention plans and adjust as needed. The market place is dynamic and plans are not set in stone. Therefore, you should be able to adjust your plan as needed.

A measurement plan should be designed to qualify your performance in terms of the return of investment of the most critical components of the marketing strategy. There are several metrics you can use to measure all the way from the business performance and effectiveness of your marketing efforts to customer satisfaction.[1] It requires resourcefulness and some technical expertise to build a good performance plan. There is a big market research and data industry built to help brands understand how they perform in market relative to competition. However, that doesn't mean you can only build a measurement plan if you hire a market research firm.

Regardless of the level of sophistication you can afford, the first and most important criteria to establish for a measurement plan is getting clear on the marketing strategy variables most crucial for success. Second is knowing how you will adjust the plan based on the data collected. Once you have identified the core metrics to track, you can work on designing a measurement plan based on the resources available.

Measurement plans should be crafted to meet the desired review and decision-making cycle. As you develop a measurement plan you should think about the actions that you will take based on the data. Will you take action based on the results? When is it time to reach out for help if you are off track? How will you rally the organization to course correct and build a new plan if needed? Those are the questions that building a performance plan will force you to do and you should do that prior to launching your plans in market. You will gain response time and peace of mind knowing that you will have a course of action to manage through the changing market conditions once your plan is in market.

If it is your first time building a measurement and performance plan for a marketing plan, here is some guidance on how you can measure the brand growth variables we have discussed throughout the book.

There are three core steps to building a measurement plan:

* Selecting the most critical metrics. These are the marketing inputs or consumer and business outputs you are relying on to deliver your growth

strategy. You must identify the metrics that tell you whether or not those variables are on the right track.

- Choosing the measurement time horizon and the frequency of review. Determine whether there is a multi-year plan or a one-year plan with monthly or quarterly expectations in your measurement plan. The core metrics that you decide to measure your success on will grow over time, thus you should have a time horizon to measure them against. Also, break down the overall goal into tangible short-term goals that you can measure gradual progress.

- Deciding how to act with the data and contingency plan. Establishing a set of actions that you will take based on the data. This will serve as your contingency plan.

At a thirty thousand foot view, a brand's growth plan will be measured by core performance metrics such as sales, market share, and profit. These are the metrics you promised at the beginning of your marketing plan. These metrics are independent as they encompass different aspects of the brand, but are also interconnected so it is worth tracking each of them separately and studying their relationship. However, there are also several marketing strategy variables that you can track as diagnostics of your likelihood to stay on track to deliver your overall goals and your brand vision.

STEP 1: SELECTING THE CORE METRICS

There are three types of metrics that you should consider tracking to measure success of your brand–building plan:

- Business Performance
- Consumer Fundamentals
- Marketing Mix Effectiveness

Business performance metrics are ways of testing the progress of the goals you set in Step 1 of the Star Brand framework. Specific metrics such as sales, market share, and profit will help you judge your brand's strategy success. Consumer fundamentals metrics intend to capture consumers' response to the products or services the brand offers in regards to appeal, value, and loyalty resulting in trial and repeat. Marketing Mix Effectiveness measures how effective each component is against its expectation and the value it adds to the overall marketing mix.

Let's explore the different ways in which you can build these metrics. If you are already managing a brand, you probably already have metrics from performance evaluation reports or the finance or market research department. Definitely consider using them for your plan if they come from a reliable and steady source.

Business Performance Metrics—Tracking Sales, Market Share, Profit

Sales are probably the easiest metric to track business performance. It is simply the output of how much product or services you sold in a given time period. To arrive at a sales amount in currency terms, simply multiply the amount of volume sold times the price at which it was sold. Each brand can measure sales differently depending on how the operations are run and the standard metrics the brand uses to count units or service sold.

Sales = unit volume x price

Measuring market share is more difficult than measuring sales because you need to know how the total market is doing and how well your competitors are doing to determine how well you are performing relative to them. To calculate market share you need to take the unit sales of your brands and divide them by the total market unit sales.

Brand market share = brand unit sales (#)/ market unit sales

To measure market share you can buy market sales data from market data providers. Nielsen, for example, offers robust market data that is extrapolated from real product purchase scans at the store level and also on a consumer panel that helps estimate the approximate market share of each key competitor in a category. If you don't have access to this kind of data, you can use other methods to determine total market sales and then your brand's ratio. There are industry reports that can be found online that can help estimate total market size for a specific industry and across different geographies. Since you already know how many units you are selling, you can use your number and divide it by the market size estimate that you gathered from secondary data. That percentage can work as a proxy of the brand's current market share position.

If secondary data is not available, you will have to be even more empirical to assess relative ratio of the market share that your brand owns. For example, you can observe how well you are doing versus competition by comparing the relative ratio of shelf space that you can own at a particular retailer. A brand with more shelf space is likely to do better than the next competitor. You can also do a relative comparison of other comparative consumer metrics such as consumer reviews or client feedback versus your brand.

If you can't measure market share because you don't have access to the rest of the market place performance, focus on your sales target versus the previous year as the main metric of performance to measure progress against. If your sales are growing and are potentially ahead of competition, it is very likely you are also growing market share.

Profit is part of the brand's core financial metrics and critical to track to ensure your growth plan is profitable. The number one driver of a brand's profit is more consumers buying the product. However, expenses associated with the creation and promotion of the products or service should be capped at a level where you deliver a profit margin. Recall that Star Brands are lucrative.

In order to measure profit, you need to be able to measure not only sales, but also how much you are spending in order to get these sales. So it is common to track total brand profit as well as the profit margin that results from each product or service sold. The profit margin is what you will make after you pay for your expenses including marketing expenditure. This metric will help make decisions on pricing, marketing spending, and profitability goals in general. It will also tell you how much more money you can generate by growing sales. Here are a couple of the most commonly used metrics to help track brand profit resulting from the sales generated:

Margin%: (unit price - unit cost) / unit cost

Total costs: Fixed cost + Total Variable cost
(unit volume x variable cost per unit)

Total Marketing cost: Marketing Fixed cost + Total Marketing Variable cost
(unit volume x variable cost per unit)

Marketing % of sales: Marketing Spending/ Revenue

Break-even volume: fixed cost / (sell price per unit – variable cost per unit)

Consumer Fundamental Metrics

It is important for a brand to measure how appealing consumers find its product or service. Consumer metrics are associated with how well the consumer is responding to the product in terms of perceived appeal, value, likelihood of continued purchase, and level of loyalty. Trial and repeat are main metrics to track but there are several other consumer metrics that help diagnose how your brand is perceived by consumers. These metrics can also be used as diagnostics of how well you are progressing towards your desired ultimate brand destination.

Trial & Repeat

To deliver on your brand sales goals you need aggressive trial levels and healthy repeat rates. So when you are setting your brand sales goals, you should also calculate how many people need to buy the product to meet the goal. This will give you an idea of roughly how many people you need to make aware of your brand, reach with your message and convince to buy.

Once you have set a trial goal for the brand's specific sales goal, you can buy the trial data to track over certain periods of time. To measure trial in market, brands can buy access to databases that will tell them approximately how many consumers have bought the brand in a given time period. Databases such as Nielsen or Dunnhumby are built based on actual behavior from consumers shopping at actual stores that is then extrapolated to the total population.

The level of repeat of the product is the sign of how well the product is delivering on the expectation of the consumer. Similar to trial, repeat can be measured via accessing databases that will tell you roughly how many of your first time buyers of the product have bought the product. Measuring it in market will let you know if you need to make adjustments to the product experience.

Appeal

Brand sales growth can only happen if consumers find your brand proposition appealing to buy. Recall appeal is one of the core variables in the brand math equation. The higher the appeal of a product or service, the more it will sell. So it is the brand manager's job to maximize the attractiveness and potential of the product or service they offer.

In order to increase the appeal of a brand, you need to understand how interested consumers are in buying it. You can learn about this prior to launching the product in market or after it is launched. If you can, you should measure how strong the appeal of the product is prior to launching in market. This includes asking the target consumers how much they like the product, its perceived quality and value, and their purchase interest.

Pre-Market Testing: To measure appeal prior to the market launch you can conduct market research by selecting a few consumers to expose to the product or service proposition and get feedback. This can be done qualitatively, with a few consumers, or quantitatively with a larger consumer sample. If you hire a research supplier, they can help you find the right consumers that represent your target and design a study that tells you how strong the appeal of your proposition is.

Quantitatively, the appeal of your brand or a product in particular can be measured via market research surveys that record consumers' purchase interest. This shows how likely consumers are to buy your product or service proposition. In market research surveys purchase interest is measured via a five-point scale question, with "definitely would buy" and "probably might buy" being the top answers that consumers can select when exposed to your brand proposition.

If you don't have a lot of resources to test your product or communication via a quantitative market study, you can use less expensive research tools today like small online forums where consumers give their opinion in exchange for an incentive or simply share the idea with a few consumers you have access to. For example, in a consumer group setting you can share any work in progress stimulus to get feedback on your proposition. It could be a concept written on paper that captures the benefit, price, and value of the product or service, the messaging you are planning to communicate and/or the actual prototype of the product or a sample for the consumer to experience. The risk with this approach is that the opinion of a few consumers won't represent the complete population of consumers who might be interested in buying the product, however it can give you some insight into how consumers perceive the proposition so you can refine it and increase your success rate.

By gathering feedback on your product proposition prior to launching, you can find out the value that consumers see in your product, how well they liked the product, how persuasive the communication is and finally how likely they are to buy it based on the stimulus they were exposed to. This will better inform the messaging and product choices for a particular launch prior to locking in your final proposition.

Plan this consumer exposure early in the development of your branded proposition so that you can actually act on the feedback and insight you gather to optimize your launch. It is much better to ask for input early in the product and communication development process, than launch the product in the market and incur significant expenses without any feedback from your potential customers. For complex product launches such as breakthrough new products, Star Brands typically spend a significant amount of time, sometimes years, talking to consumers and testing the proposition until they have arrived at the most valuable proposition. This approach typically takes a lot of dollars and resources but can be worth it if the investment in launching the product is significant.

In-Market Testing: If the product is already in market, to measure appeal, you can conduct customer satisfaction surveys to ask consumers questions such as how well they like the product, how they are using it, how likely they are to continue using it and so on. You can uncover what they like and dislike about the product and any opportunities to improve their experience.

If you can't conduct full market research, sometimes listening to transcripts of the 1800 line of your product, online reviews, or Facebook posts (if your brand is available in social media) can give you insight into overall satisfaction of the product. If your product is not meeting the expectations of the customer who bought it, you will eventually find out.

Loyalty

Loyalty is defined as consumers continuing to prefer your brand over others as they believe your brand products or services are superior to other competitive offerings. To measure loyalty means measuring the strength of this relationship the consumer has with the brand over time. Since this could be a very subjective measure, you can break it down into the types of behaviors and attitudes that loyal customers typically exhibit. Here are some examples:

* Superior perception of your brand's value and quality
* Larger number and quantities of the purchases made
* Higher-than-average length of the relationship over time
* Willingness to buy additional products or services from the brand
* High level of advocacy and likelihood of recommending the brand

Measuring how your brand is doing against some of these consumers' attitudes or behaviors will give you a good idea of the level of loyalty the brand generates. If you have purchasing data, you can probably analyze the number of consumers that are repurchasing and the frequency. Also, online consumer comments can tell you what the most loyal consumers are saying about the brand or why some decide to abandon you.

Strive to find your loyal consumers and learn from them. They will help you manage your brand better. Talking to loyal consumers can give you great insight into the most valuable traits of your brand and what is working best. These sets of consumers can be the most honest in giving you feedback when you are looking to make a major product, packaging, or communication change. If you are considering changing any core element of your brand strategy, consult with them.

Marketing Mix Effectiveness

The effectiveness of the marketing mix determines how many consumers are persuaded to try your product. The core metric to measure the effectiveness of your marketing mix is return on investment (ROI). That is the return on the investment of every dollar you put into the marketing mix equation in terms of generating actual sales. What drives marketing ROI is how well each of the marketing mix variables contributes to generating sales. Tracking each component will give you great interim diagnostics as a proxy of how likely you are to deliver your sales target. If your marketing plan is not working well in market, the symptoms of an ill performance will be visible.

There are very sophisticated statistical models that can measure the effectiveness of your marketing spend by analyzing historical periods of performance. These models can explain how effective each of the marketing mix vehicles you choose, are contributing to your overall sales. The output of these models can give you a quantified ROI calculation by vehicle. With this ROI calculation you can fine tune the marketing mix for the brand and adjust investment levels as needed.

In the absence of a statistic model, you can use the brand math formula and populate it with the data that you have available to arrive at a proxy of how each variable is impacting brand sales. You can also set a pre and post period of your market results for when the marketing activity will take place. Having a pre and post activity period will allow you to attribute any changes in your sales or market share to the specific marketing execution that is in market. The pre-period should be a stable time frame of business results when you didn't have the communication in market compared to a stable post period during in which your communication has been in market.

While there are a lot more variables other than marketing that can affect your results, you can generally find a correlation in the post period with the marketing activity when you time your measurements correctly. In the post period you expect sales to have increased as a result of your investment in media and your message. If this is the case, simply continue doing what is working. If the post period doesn't show improvement, you need to dig deeper on each of the marketing vehicles, and the communication in particular, to understand why it is not effective and adjust accordingly.

Awareness

A great metric to measure how well your market mix, and in particular your media and messaging, is working is brand awareness. The number of people who become aware of your brand or your particular message will tell you how effective marketing strategy is in market. Similar to market share, measuring awareness requires understanding where your brand and message ranks in the mind of consumers versus other competitive messages. For example, you want your brand to be the first one that comes to mind to consumers. If you ask a consumer, "What brand comes to mind when you think 'cookie'?" a brand like Oreo would want to be the first brand that comes to mind for the consumer, especially since their messaging is all about being the "world's favorite cookie." This is called top-of-mind awareness and it can be measured via market research.

To measure awareness, you need to conduct a market study to ask a representative sample of consumers if they have ever heard of your brand and also what are all other brands associated with the category. Only by knowing the full list will you know how well your brand ranks. Several research suppliers offer awareness tracking and media tracking services to measure brand awareness in a specific point in time or ongoing.

If you are investing significant dollars in media, you should definitely carve out the dollars to measure your brand awareness. Similar to sales measurement, you can establish monthly or quarterly awareness goals that you need to meet as a metric of how many consumers you are effectively reaching to deliver your long-term business goal.

Media and Message Effectiveness

Your anticipated marketing effectiveness might be affected by other messages in the market place and by the competition. Thus, you need to be able to quickly understand if the message is effective in market and adjust accordingly—that can be by editing your ads, pulling them from market, or creating new ones.

Recall awareness is impacted by the quality of the message and the type of media that you buy. Strong creative messaging is a core driver of marketing ROI, so you should measure its quality. However, the quality of your messaging is best measured in market. This is for two reasons. First, there is a lot of magic that can happen once a message is executed well across touch points and is proven superior in market. Second, the relevancy of the media vehicle that you choose for the message will also affect its effectiveness.

To measure media and message effectiveness in market, you can commission market research surveys that can tell you how many consumers recall the brand, the messaging, and how persuaded they were to buy after being exposed to the advertising. Also, whether you work via a media-buying agency or buy media directly from the market place, the media provider can offer data as to how and where the media that you bought was delivered. Always consider the quality of the messaging as well as the quality of the media you bought as core diagnostics for the specific awareness and trial goals that you have set for the brand.

If you are interested in measuring the message effectiveness prior to launch you can do some pre-market testing like focus groups or quantitative copy testing where consumers get exposed to your ad in a controlled environment. Pre-market testing for communication works well when you are trying to screen down options from several pieces of advertising by exposing them to the target groups while in progress. Think of pre-market testing for advertising as diagnostic tools versus measuring potential. So the input you get can help make the message clearer or more distinctive. Don't rely on pre-market advertising testing to determine how effective the media and messaging will ultimately be in market.

Distribution

Distribution, a core element of the marketing mix, can be measured in a couple of ways. A straight calculation of distribution could be the number of physical stores or points of sale; the product is distributed across all the retail channels you are in. This applies to points of sale that the brand owns, or its retailers or distributors that carry the brand. However, this measure won't capture how effective those points of sale are, it will only give you a relative measure of the breadth of availability your brand has.

Another way to measure distribution is to quantify the availability of products sold through retailers or re-sellers as a percentage of all potential outlets. The common industry metric to measure distribution this way is called all-commodity volume (value) or ACV. The ACV is typically measured as a percentage of the total dollar sales that are available in a retail channel. The total volume that is included in the ACV metric includes the entire store inventory sales, rather than sales for a specific category of products—hence the term "all commodity volume." ACV is then a more accurate measure of how available your product is considering the size of the market. If your brand is in the consumer goods category and is sold at retailers like Walmart or Target, you can likely purchase your ACV data from market measurement providers for your tracking purposes. Sales teams are rewarded based on how well they grow distribution and influence this measure, thus they will commonly track it as well.

ACV: Total sales of stores carrying the brand/ all store sales

Pricing

If you don't have exact control over the final pricing the consumer pays for your product, it is a good idea to track the pricing in the marketplace. There are databases you can access for average pricing information if your product is tracked via panel data. If not, simply compare prices online or where your product is available and track the averages. You want the product to hold the intended market pricing.

Usage

Monitoring your product consumption is helpful to understand the rates at which consumers buy your product. This could be the number of units per purchase, frequency of purchase, preferred quantities, etc. Panel data or actual transaction data is the most reliable way to measure it.

STEP 2: SELECTING THE TIME PERIODS

Once you have selected the metrics that you will care most about you need to decide when to measure them, the time period to measure each of them on, and how frequently you will review them. As a brand manager you can't afford to wait a full year to know whether your plan is on track or not. In order to know if the level of sales you are getting is on track versus the overall business goal over time, you should try to break the ultimate sales goal target into shorter periods of time. This way you will be able to reconcile the current results of the particular growth variable you are measuring versus expectations and make decisions on the appropriate resource allocation. The intent is that you can track ongoing the market and consumer response to the specific marketing efforts you deploy instead of waiting a whole year to see how everything worked.

Breaking down your goals into a shorter measurement time frame will make them more trackable. For example, let's think of a marketing plan for a soft drink brand that is built to deliver a one-year sales increase of 10 percent. You really can't wait a full year to determine whether you are on track or not. You can easily turn the annual goal into a monthly goal, even a weekly goal if needed so you can better track progress. If you are off track for the first few months, let's say only growing sales at 2 percent, it is very possible you won't meet your annual goal. Knowing early that you could be off track will help you adjust the plans to get back on track.

Monthly goal setting will give you the right signal of how well your plans are working in market and give you the time to make adjustments to course correct. Determine how can you break down your core metrics into shorter periods of time so that you can keep a pulse on them and monitor progress.

Frequency of Review

Decide upfront how often you will read your metrics. Set your metrics on a schedule of when they will be reviewed based on the best data available. Not all data measurement will be available at the same time. Sales in theory could be measured daily, but more complicated consumer metrics like awareness or loyalty might be available on a quarterly or annual basis depending on the tools you use.

If achieving a particular level of share is critical to your marketing plan, schedule a metrics review as often as the data becomes available. If you need to assess progress every month, be clear which metrics will be available and what you will judge your progress on.

Align the measurement frequency and review timeline with the key stakeholders to which you owe a progress report. It is common to have formal reviews of how the marketing plan is tracking versus expectations and discuss any courses of action. If the measurement reviews are conducted as a team, that is the opportunity to discuss ideas on how to adjust the plan if performance is falling short. If they are conducted with management, they are an opportunity to seek guidance and request help or call out any risk on the ongoing viability of the plan.

STEP 3: DECIDING HOW TO ACT WITH THE DATA AND CONTINGENCY PLAN

A measurement plan without action steps is just data. More important than the data itself is determining what type of actions you will consider taking based on the assessment of that particular metric. This will help you and your team react more quickly to what is going on in market and stay on track to deliver your ultimate business growth goal. This is often called Contingency Planning or Risk Management Planning.

Once you have the right metrics laid out in a measurement schedule, create potential marketplace scenarios and plan your courses of action. By doing this you will be able to identify trigger points to take action based on how your core metrics are tracking versus expectations. Set these actions ahead of time so that you are ready to act once the data is available. It will also serve as pre-alignment with your team on the potential course of action, which will make any adjustment to the plan. You will gain agility so that adjustments happen more quickly.

The output of the measurement can signal different courses of action. The action taken if your share number is half of what was expected might be different than the one taken when you are exceeding your target. Therefore, it is helpful to organize your actions based on how the particular metric is tracking versus expectations. The extent and significance of the action you take should be consistent with how big or small the difference is between the actual metric and the expectation. The more off-track you are, the more drastic the intervention required will be to return to the goal.

Use your business understanding and the whole set of data at hand to decide when it is better to continue to monitor results that are below expectations or immediately act on them. For example, if your sales are lower than expected for three consecutive meaningful periods, you might need an intervention plan. Perhaps taking action after just one review period is too soon. You want to understand if lower-than-expected performance is a trend or a one-time blip. Then, depending on the health of the other metrics, you can determine whether only one particular variable needs attention or several of them (which could be the sign of a larger problem).

Conversely, if your sales are ahead of what you expected, you should be building a plan to fuel the momentum or stay the course. Make sure all other key variables are on track as well. Remember that the best way to manage risk is to have a contingency plan.

At the end of this chapter, you'll find an example of a brand measurement plan that goes along the U. S. Harley Davidson marketing plan presented in the previous chapter. The selected metrics and goals are relevant and specific to the Harley Davidson business. They will vary from plan to plan and brand to brand. This plan includes the cumulative goal as well as shorter term goals, which is the ultimate goal broken down in smaller periods of time to make it easier to monitor. You see how the monthly and quarterly goals build up to a cumulative annual goal.

You will also notice that this brand measurement plan includes a contingency table. For a specific period of review, in this case monthly, there are potential action steps assigned per metric depending on how they will perform versus expectations. These sets of actions serve as a contingency plan. These can also be further prioritized based on their relative impact in achieving the brand's success. You can use a measurement plan like this for ongoing tracking, management reviews, and also in your marketing plan document.

SUMMARY

You are now well-versed on how the different components of marketing strategy come together to grow a brand and how you can measure progress towards the established goals in the marketing plan.

We wrapped up all five steps of the Star Brand Model into one tangible business proposal to build your brand in the next year. However, note that even if the marketing plan is typically built and tracked for one performance year, you need to always think about the brand strategy in broader terms and a longer time horizon. It will likely require several marketing plans and adjustments along the way to effectively move your brand from the current state to its ideal vision. That is the challenging and yet exciting task of any brand manager.

Congratulations!

You have completed all five steps of the Star Brand Model! You are now well equipped with the right tools and theory you need to build, market, and manage a Star Brand.

Now go and make it happen!

Brand Measurement plan — Harley Davidson Bikes 2015

	GOAL METRIC	ANNUAL GOAL	MONTHLY	CURRENT
Brand/ Business				
Sales/ Revenue	Dollar Sales	$110MM	$9,170MM	
Unit Sales	Volume Sales	55,000	4,583	
Market Share	Market position vs. competition	45%	1%	
Marketing Spending	Level of spending	$20MM	$5MM/ quarter	
Gross Margin	% per item sold	15%	15%	
Profit	Total profit or % profit per item sold	$38.5 MM	$9.625MM /quarter	
Consumer Metrics				
Trial	First time purchasers or % of population	49,000	4, 083	
Repeat	Second+ time purchasers	6,000	500	
Appeal	Purchase interest, Perceived value (Protype testing and Test Drive Feedback)	75% interested in purchasing		
Loyalty	Length of relationship, Advocacy, Customer satisfaction	HIGH HOG Advocacy; 100 Active Brand advocates		
Marketing Mix				
ROI	Marketing ROI, Diagnostic per vehicle	$3.00		
Awareness	Brand or message awareness	60%	50%/ first 6 months	
Media/ Message Quality	Advertising scores, media tracking	As strong as previous campaign		
Distribution	Store Distribution / ACV	95%		
Volume per customer	Average transaction volume	1.1		
Pricing	Average Retail Price	$20M	$20M	
Competition Performance	Market Share, Pricing Delta	105 Price Index vs. competition	105 price index	

ACTIONS & CONTIGENCY PLAN

Ahead of expectation	As expected	Below expectation
Reinvest in top vehicles	Opporutnities to grow further	Identify causes (marketing mix or product) & Adjust spending
Reinvest in top vehicles	Opporutnities to grow further	Identify causes (marketing mix or product) & Adjust spending
Reinvest in top vehicles	Opporutnities to grow further	Identify causes (marketing mix or product) & Adjust spending
Cap spending	Develop Upside spending scenarios	Understand causes and adjust
Focus on Trial	Identify opportunity to reduce costs	Revisit cost structure
Focus on Trial	Identify opportunity to reduce costs	Revisit cost structure or sales drivers
Focus on Trial	identify trial barriers	Identify trial barriers and consider promotion tactics
Increase support of HOG activities	Opportunities to strenghten engagement	Targeted effort @ HOGs incl Lifestyle & apparel
Increase spending on most effective vehicles	Identify opportunities to strenghten	Identify causes (marketing mix or product) & address
Turn loyals into ambassadors	Identify opportunities to strenghten	Review customer feedback & address
Increase marketing spending	Opportunities to optimize further	Re-invest in only vehicles that are working. Stop others or improve them
Focus on driving Trial	Assess most/ least effective channels	Re-evaluate messaging and vehicles choices
Maximize opportunities to dissemiminate the message. Invest in more media	Assess most/ least effective channels and messaging	Not air, re-work creative or re-brief
Focus on Trial	Identify expansion opportunities	Close distribution gaps
Focus on trial	Opportunity to improve transaction size	Offer incentives to increase purchase
Analyze sales impact and adjust	Identify oppportunity to trade customers up	Analyze sales, financial impact and adjust
Analyze competitiveness	Analyze competitiveness	Revisit financial impact and adjust

Acknowledgments

"When you are inspired by some great purpose, some extraordinary project, all your thoughts break their bounds. Your mind transcends limitations, your consciousness expands in every direction and you find yourself in a new, great, and wonderful world. Dormant forces, faculties, and talents become alive."
~ Patanjali

THANK YOU!

Debbie Millman, without whom this book wouldn't be possible

Myles Gaythwaite, the best designer I could have wished for

Andres Mongrue, great partner and rising star of the media world

All my students from SVA Masters in Branding 2012, 2013, 2014 classes, especially Olivia Barry and Alison Ketchledge who helped edit the book

All contributors: Paul Smith, Professor Amitava Chattopadhyay, Jim Stengel, Lynne Gordon, many others, and all the Star Brands featured

All my great bosses, coaches, and mentors over the years at Procter & Gamble

My family and friends who were incredibly supportive during my long writing weekends

Glossary

Accountability: Assuming complete responsibility for understanding brand strategy, advertising, budget and ultimately the market sales.

Analysis and Measurement: Analyzing market performance with personal investigation of business results, retailers, and consumers trends.

Appeal: In regards to brands, how attractive the product or service they offer is for people to buy.

Attractive Segment: A segment that is sizable enough to meet a brand's sales growth expectations.

Benefits: A core element of any brand communication; also reflected in the equity pyramid; a statement that captures the basis upon the brand expects consumers to select the advertised product.

Brand Assessment and Goal Setting: Step 1 of the Star Brand Model to determine where a brand currently stands (brand and market assessment) and its ultimate destination (vision and goals).

Brand Awareness: The number of people in the national population that know a particular brand exists and recognize what it stands for.

Brand Equity: Includes the overall uniqueness and perception of all the components of a brand such as strategy, communication, visual identity, products that are set in place to create value in the marketplace.

Brand Equity Health: A brand's ability as a system to attract consumers to buy products, especially in relation to other brands that it competes against.

Brand Framework/Model: A guided set of strategic choices brand managers can make on a consistent basis to build the brand and increase the odds of attracting many customers

Brand Health: Understanding both financial health, as well as the health of the brand equity as a system that has the ability to attract consumers to buy products.

Brand Ideal: The reason why the brand exists and why it creates the products and services it offers.

Brand Manager: The person responsible for the development and execution of a brand strategy seeking to grow the brand's awareness and competitiveness in the marketplace, thus its sales and market value as a result.

Brand Math Formula: Mathematical formula that expresses how the marketing mix impacts brand sales manifested in consumer trial and repeat.

Brand Promise: A statement of what the brand uniquely offers setting expectations for consumers in terms of benefits and experiences associated with its products and/or services. It can be the ultimate core benefit the brand offers to solve a consumer need and how the brand delivers on its ideal.

Brand Repeat: Number of consumers that repeat a purchase of a particular product.

Brand Target: All consumers to whom the brand's equity (in particular the brand's ideal and promise) is relevant and meaningful; typically includes one or more needs-based segments.

Brand Trial: Number of consumers that buy a particular product for the first time.

Building the Marketing Plan and Measurement: Step 5 of the Star Brand Model that consolidates all the previous steps into a tangible marketing and measurement plan to execute in market.

Business Performance Metrics: Metrics such as sales, market share, & profit.

CAGR: Compound Annual Growth Rate

Clarity: A quality of Star Brands. Understanding what you stand for, who your target is, the insights to connect with them, and the right marketing mix for effective communication.

Crafting a Communication Strategy: Step 3 of the Star Brand Model to identify benefits and insights that give birth to brand ideas and how to make them travel in media.

Commitment to Learning: A quality of Star Brands. Learning from the past and quickly adapting for the future.

Consistency: A quality of Star Brands. The look, feel, sound, and smell of how the brand intends, consistently executed, regardless of the touch point.

Consumer Fundamentals Metrics: Metrics that capture consumers' response to the products or services the brand offers in regards to appeal, value and loyalty resulting in trial and repeat.

CPGs: Consumer Product Goods companies

Defining Brand Equity and Target: Step 2 of the Star Brand Model to define what the brand will stand for in the market place and select the brand target to focus all efforts on.

Equity Pyramid: Visual representation of a brand's core components; brand ideal; brand promise; unique benefits (that set the brand apart), and ownable assets.

Establishing the Marketing Strategy: Step 4 of the Star Brand Model to develop the right marketing mix to achieve the brand's goals.

Executional Leadership: A quality of brand managers. Leading with excellence the planning and execution of brand activities.

Financial health: Meeting, and hopefully exceeding, the expectations of the brand's investors.

Four "Ps": Product, price, promotion and place; explain marketing as the activity that puts the right product, at the right place, at the right price, at the right time. Components of marketing mix.

Growth Strategy: Pursued to yield higher sales versus year ago, improve the brands market share position and ideally maintain—if not improve—the overall profit structure of the brand.

Harvesting Strategy: Used when a business that doesn't have long-term potential or the brand has lost significant competitive advantage, yet still delivers positive cash flow and profit; also commonly referred to as a "milking" strategy.

Higher Order Purpose: A quality of Star Brands. An ideal that a brand seeks to contribute to the world.

IBI: Insights, Benefits, Ideas. Components of the brand's communication strategy.

Ideas: A core element of any brand communication; the transformation of the communication strategy into a compelling and interesting expression to be executed in an advertising format across marketing touch points.

Insights: A core element of any brand communication; an accurate, deep intuitive understanding of a human truth. In the case of a brand, a consumer insight is a discovery of an inconspicuous human truth, often combining bits of knowledge, and actionable via a tension that touches the consumer's heart.

Internal Assessment: Diagnostic exercise to capture how internal stakeholders, everyone from the CEO down to hourly employees, or business partners if it is a start up, currently perceive the brand.

Learning Organization: A term first coined by MIT scientist Peter Senge; an organization that facilitates the learning of its members to expand their thinking capacity, allowing them to better adapt to the changing market conditions and evolve over time.

Loyalty: Consumers continuing to prefer one brand over another, as they believe that brand of products or services are superior to other competitive offerings.

Market Assessment: Diagnostic exercise to articulate how the brand is perceived in relation to its competition in the marketplace and external factors.

Marketing Mix: The combination of factors such as resources and market tactics, represented by the "Four Ps", that can be controlled by a brand to influence consumers to purchase its products or services.

Marketing Mix Effectiveness: Measures how effective each component is against its expectation and the value it adds to the overall marketing mix.

Marketing Plan: A physical document and process to solidify the brand's marketing strategy and the plans to execute against.

Marketing Strategy: The process of creating a plan to deliver the brand's goals of increasing sales and building sustainable brand value

Measurement Plan: Helps track how a plan is performing versus the ultimate goal and provides diagnostic measures of likelihood of success and/or areas that need intervention.

Media: The primary method brands use to get their branding and messaging in front of the right people in the right place and at the right time.

Media Planning: Selecting the best media vehicles to reach the consumer and budgeting for the amount of media needed to reach the brand's desired media objectives such as awareness, engagement, etc.

Needs: The main reason why a consumer enters or buys a category of products and/or services and makes a specific brand and variant selection.

Needs Based Segment: A homogenous group of consumers whose needs/ drivers of brand and variant choice are different from other consumers.

OOH: Out-of-home

Operational Discipline: Making a plan and budget, executing that plan, and then measuring the results for improved and future action

Opportunities: External factors the brand can capitalize on to grow the business.

Placement: The physical or virtual place where the product or service can be purchased. A component of the marketing mix. Also referred to as distribution.

Points of Difference: Benefits a brand offers and excels at and therefore strives to own in the market place.

Points of Parity: Benefits a brand offers that might be important but not superior versus competition.

Price: The monetary amount a consumer pays for the product or service the brand offers.

Product: The physical good or service offered to the customer. A component of the marketing mix.

Profit: The money that is left after paying for all expenses, people, products, and employees.

Promotion: All communications and tactics used to encourage consumers to buy a product or service. A component of the marketing mix.

Protect and Defend Strategy: Used when market dynamics have changed and are threatening the brand's ability to deliver sustained sales, share, profit, and long-term growth.

Receptivity: When and where consumers are most disposed to receive a specific category and brand message.

Sales Growth: Typically the main measure of brand growth. Often expressed as a percentage of gross sales during a determined period versus the same period of the previous year(s).

Sampling: Promotional tactic. Smaller size product or length of service that gives the consumer the opportunity to try before committing to the purchase, thus reducing the brand's trial barrier.

Segmenting: A way of organizing your universe of customers into meaningful and distinct groups.

SMART: Specific, Measurable, Actionable, Realistic, and Timely. Acronym used to qualify goals and objectives.

Star Brands: Admired brands that successfully connect with the hearts and minds of their customers and achieve growing sales, profit, and market leadership over time. These brands exhibit the following core qualities: clarity; consistency; higher-order purpose; emotional connection; superior benefits; commitment to learning.

Strengths: Internal factors and capabilities that offer a brand a competitive edge to succeed in market.

Sub-segment: Subset of the brand target or needs based segment that represents the greatest near term growth potential; typically used for short-term marketing initiatives.

Superior Benefits: Benefits a brand offers that excels to set it apart from its competition.

Sustain Strategy: Implies more measured and consistent growth; likely more applicable to a mature category and/or years when the brand doesn't have any major product innovation or funds available to grow expansively.

SWOT Analysis: An analysis tool that helps organize a brand's strengths, weaknesses, opportunities, and threats.

Target: The uniquely defined and selected type of customer that a brand focuses on to attract and delight.

Threats: External factors that might affect the brand in the near or long-term future.

Top of Mind Awareness: Number of consumers for whom a specific brand first comes to mind when asked about brands in any given industry.

Trial Barrier: A specific brand challenge and reason why consumers aren't buying a product.

Vision: The desired brand growth trajectory and ultimate destination of a brand.

Weaknesses: Internal factors that could stop or slow down a brand's growth and success.

Notes

Chapter 1

1 Senge, Peter M. *The Fifth Discipline: The Art & Practice of The Learning Organization.* Random House, 2010. Kindle edition.

Chapter 2

1 Dyer, Davis, Frederick Dalzell , and Rowena Olegario. *Rising Tide: Lessons from 165 Years of Brand Building* at Procter & Gamble. Boston: Harvard Business Review Press, 2004

2 Brand Rants; The McElroy "Brand Man" Memo turns 80" blog entry by Sean Duffy, May 11 2011 http://www.brandrants.com/brandrants/2011/05/mcelroy-brand-man-memo.html

3 Branding Strategy Insider; "Great Moments In Branding: Neil McElroy Memo" blog entry by Derrick Daye, June 12th, 2009. http://www.brandingstrategyinsider.com/2009/06/great-moments-in-branding-neil-mcelroy-memo.html#.U6jQCvldUuc

4 Vollmer, Christopher, and Geoffrey Precourt. *Always On: Advertising, Marketing, and Media in an Era of Consumer Control.* McGraw-Hill, 2008.

5 Bill George, "Developing Mindful Leaders for the C-Suite," HBR Blog Network, March 10, 2014, http://blogs.hbr.org/2014/03/developing-mindful-leaders-for-the-c-suite/?utm_source=Socialflow&utm_medium=Tweet&utm_campaign=Socialflow

Chapter 3

1 Watkins, Michael D. The *First 90 Days. Critical Success Strategies for New Leaders at All levels.* Boston: Harvard Business School Press, 2003

Chapter 4

1 The website of Starbucks; "Starbucks Heritage"; www.starbucks.com/about-us/our-heritage

2 The website of Lego; "The Lego Brand". http://aboutus.lego.com/en-us/lego-group/the_lego_brand

Chapter 5

1 Keller, Kevin Lane. Jim Stengel (Author) Building, Measuring, and Managing Brand Equity. New Jersey: Pearson Education 2003.

2 Maslow, Abraham H. "A theory of human motivation." Psychological Review (1943): 50(4), 370–96, accessed April 10, 2014 http://psychclassics.yorku.ca/Maslow/motivation.htm

3 Conley, Chip. *Peak: How Great Companies Get Their Mojo from Maslow.* San Francisco: Jossey- Bass 2007

4 Jim Stengel (author of *Grow: How Ideals Power Growth and Profit at the World's Greatest Companies*) in discussion with the author, March 2014.

5 Olsen, Erica. "Strategic Planning: Positioning Statement Examples" in *Strategic Planning Kit For Dummies.* John Wiley and Sons, 2012. Kindle Edition

6 New Kind; "Kevin Keller's five favorite classic brand mantras" blog entry by Chris Gramms, October 2011 http://newkind.com/kevin-kellers-five-favorite-classic-brand-mantras/

7 Nolan, Richard L, and Suresh Kotha. "Harley Davidson: Preparing for the Next Century". Case Study. Harvard Business School, March 14, 2006.

Chapter 6

1 Amitava Chattopadhyay (The GlaxoSmithKline Chaired Professor in Corporate Innovation at INSEAD), in discussion with the author, February 2014.

2 Chattopadhyay, Amitava, and Rajeev Batra with Aysegul Ozsomer, *The New Emerging Market Multinationals: Four Strategies for Disrupting Markets and Building Brands.* McGrawHill 2012.

3 The website Mahindra & Mahindra USA; "Why Mahindra"; www.mahindrausa.com/Why-mahindra

4 Best, Roger J. Market-Based Management: Strategies for Growing Customer Value Profitability. New Jersey: Pearson Prentice Hall, 2005

5 Smith, Paul. *Lead with a Story: A Guide to Crafting Business Narratives that Captivate, Convince, and Inspire.* American Management Association, 2012. Kindle Edition.

6 Paul Smith (Storytelling coach and author of the best selling book Lead with a Story), in discussion with the author, January 2014.

Chapter 7

1 Cleese, John. "What drives Creativity", YouTube video March 2012 https://www.youtube.com/watch?v=ijtQP9nwrQA

2 "Dove Camera Shy Campaign. Press release". Unilever, accessed January 17, 2014, www.prnewswire.com/news-releases/dove-camera-shy-exposes-a-universal-

truth-214174461.html
3 The Gentleman's Log, "Sport Club Recife: Immortal Fans" blog entry by Chris Rawlinson June 18th, 2013, www.chrisrawlinson.com/2013/06/sport-club-recife-immortal-fans/
4 The website of Master Card; "Consumer Marketing Initiatives"; http://www.mastercard.com/us/company/en/whatwedo/consumer_marketing.html
5 Kevin Allen, "Win the Pitch: Tips from MasterCard's "Priceless" Pitchman" HBR Blog Network, May 8, 2012, http://blogs.hbr.org/2012/05/mastering-the-art-of-the-pitch/
6 Lynne Gordon (Chief Executive Brandtone Africa) in discussion about Carling Black Label "Be the Champion Coach" Campaign, October 2013

Chapter 8

1 Kantar Media Strategy multimedia ad expenditure database across all measured media, accessed May 15, 2014.
2 Jack Neff, "Unilever Ad Spending Hits New Heights, But Agency Fees on Downward Trend" AdAge, January 23rd, 2013, http://adage.com/article/news/unilever-ad-spending-hits-heights/239348/
3 Wittebols, James H, *Watching M★A★S★H, Watching America: A Social History of the 1972-1983 Television Series*, McFarland 2003
4 The website of the The Nielsen Company; Nielsen Top Ten TV Shows Week of July 7, 2014 http://www.nielsen.com/content/corporate/us/en/top10s.html
5 eMarkter Worldwide Ad Spending Report; "Global Ad Spending Growth To Double This Year" July 9, 2014 http://www.emarketer.com/Article/Global-Ad-Spending-Growth-Double-This-Year/1010997
6 2013 Q3 Nielsen Global Adview Pulse Lite accessed January 22, 2014 http://www.nielsen.com/us/en/insights/reports/2014/global-adview-pulse-lite-q3-2013.html
7 2013 eMarketer Worldwide Ad Spending Forecast: Emerging Markets, Mobile Provide Opportunities for Growth. Full report January 2013 http://www.emarketer.com
8 2014 eMarketer. Mobile Continues to Steal Share of US Adults' Daily Time Spent with Media. April 2014. http://www.emarketer.com/Article/Mobile-Continues-Steal-Share-of-US-Adults-Daily-Time-Spent-with-Media/1010782

9 The New York Times Company; Results of The New York Times Customer Insight Group's 2013: The Year of Video Survey. October 2013. http://www.nytco.com/results-to-the-new-york-times-customer-insight-groups-2013-the-year-of-video-survey/
10 Internationalist Awards For Innovation: Silver – Chevrolet – "*Glee*-mercial" 2012. http://www.internationalist-awards.com/media_2012/chevy-glee.html
11 GFK MRI Media Audience Measurement, Consumer Insights, And Market Solutions Various consumer segmentation software pulls
12 Laura Stampler. "We Love These Vintage Ads In Newsweek's New Mad Men Issue." Business Insider. March 19, 2012. http://www.businessinsider.com/here-are-all-of-the-vintage-ads-for-newsweeks-mad-men-themed-issue-2012-3
13 Joshua Pramis. "World's Most-Visited Tourist Attractions No. 1: Times Square, New York City" Travel & Leisure Online. October 2011. http://www.travelandleisure.com/articles/worlds-most-visited-tourist-attractions/2

Chapter 9

1 "Marketing Mix", Wikipedia, last modified June 10, 2014, http://en.wikipedia.org/wiki/Marketing_mix
2 Borden, Neil. "The Concept of the Marketing Mix". Journal of Advertising Research 1984
3 Hsieh, Tony. *Delivering Happiness: A Path to Profits, Passion, and Purpose*. Business Plus, 2013. Kindle edition.

Chapter 11

1 "Harley Davidson, INC10K Statement", Harley Davidson http://ar.harley-davidson.com/
2 Nolan, Richard L, and Suresh Kotha. "Harley Davidson: Preparing for the Next Century". Case Study. Harvard Business School, March 14, 2006.

Chapter 12

1 Farris, Paul W., Neil T. Bendle, Phillip E. Pfeifer and David J. Reibstein. *Marketing Metrics: The Definitive Guide to Measuring Marketing Performance*, New Jersey: Pearson Education, 2010

Permissions

Big Mac image courtesy of © McDonald's Corp.
Coca-Cola logo and bottle design © The Coca Cola
Company.
Image of Yvon Chouinard by Tom Frost
Patagonia trademark © Patagonia Inc.
Google Maps Street View image courtesy of © Google
Espresso Image courtesy of © Starbucks Corp.
Lego mini-fig and toy duck images courtesy of © LEGO
IBM trademark and licensed articles © IBM Inc.
Renderings of Method's Pullman factory © William
McDonough+Partners
Michelin trademark and licensed articles © Michelin Inc.
Starbucks logo courtesy of © Starbucks Corp.
Harley Davidson logo and motorcycle image courtesy of
© Harley Davidson
Mahindra tractor image courtesy of © Mahindra
Perrier bottle image courtesy © Nestlé Waters
Corporation
Dove trademark and licenced articles © Unilever Inc.
Carling Black Label trademark and licenced articles ©
Carling Inc.
Tojan logo © Church & Dwight Company
Heinekin logo © Heinekin Inc
RedBull Logo © Redbull GmbH
Apple trademark and licenced articles © Apple Inc.
MasterCard trademark and articles © MasterCard Inc.
Glee screen grab © Fox & General Motors
Allstate trademark and licenced articles © Allstate Inc.
Walmart trademark and licenced articles © Walmart Inc.,
image in public domain

All other illustrations created by
Myles Gaythwaite © 2015

Index

A

Accountability, 13
Ad spends, 154
Advertisers, 138–141, 143–148, 150, 152, 153
Advertising
Apple products, 120, 121
  campaign, 119–121
  core components of, 128
  development process, 127, 131
  effective, 130
  evaluation, 130–135
  execution, 133
  as marketing strategy component, 196
  and media, 169
  mentors, 132
Advertising agency, 127, 129
All-commodity volume (value) (ACV), 215
Appeal, 179–181, 209–211
Apple, 1, 120, 121
Assets, brand
  ownable, 72–73
  recognizable, 77–79
Attractiveness, 92–95
Awareness, brand, 177–179, 213

B

Benefits, brand, 116–118
  emotional benefits, 118
  functional benefits, 118
Blogger relations, media, 149
Borden, Neil H., 166
Bottled water brands, 86–87
Brand
  assessment, 8
  assets, 72–73
  awareness, 177–179, 213
  execution, 72
  goal, 8, 194
  message, 176, 178
  objectives, 194
  packaging, 72
  role, 70
  vision exercise, 42–44
  visual identity, 73
Brand-building process, 6, 82
Brand-building tasks, 70–71

Brand equity, 59–61, 195
  core components
    brand ideal, 62–67
    brand promise, 68–69
    brand assets, 72–73
    unique benefits, 70–71
Brand equity health, 27
Brand evolution stages, 34–38
  divestiture, 38
  realignment, 37
  startup, 36
  sustaining success, 36–37
  turnaround, 37–38
Brand framework, 6
Brand health, 26
Brand ideal, 62–67
Brand management, 12
  accountability, 13
  analysis and measurement, 13
  brand advertising, 14
  collaboration, 13
  executional leadership, 13
  future of, 16
  modern, 14–16
  operational discipline, 14
  principles of, 12–13
Brand manager, 13, 29, 60, 73, 82, 90, 119, 127, 130, 131, 138, 148, 189–191
Brand math formula, variables
  appeal, 179–181
  awareness, 177–179
  distribution, 181–182
  usage, 182–184
Brand promise, 68–69
Brand repeat, 176, 208–209
Brand strategies, 48–52
  growth strategy, 50
  harvesting strategy, 51–52
  protect and defend strategy, 51
  sustain strategy, 50–51
Brand target, 195
  Mahindra & Mahindra, 82–85
  meeting and understanding, 98–103
  needs segment, 90–94
  segmenting market, 85–89
  sub-segments, 94–97

Brand trial, 129, 176, 208–209
Brown, Millward, 4, 64
Budgets, media, 139–140
    based on historical data, 154–155
    based on sales/spending ratio, 155
Business model, 2
Business performance metrics
    market share, 206
    profit, 207–208
    tracking sales, 206

C
CAGR. See Compound annual growth rate
Camay soap, 12
Carling black label case study, 123–127
Chattopadhyay, Amitava, 82
Clarity, 3
Classé Denim jeans brand, 88, 89, 92, 97
Cleese, John, 109
Coca-Cola, 1, 178
Commitment to learning, 5–6
Communication strategy, insight/benefit, 129–130
Compound annual growth rate (CAGR), 46
Consistency, 3
Consumer fundamental metrics, 206
    appeal of brand, 209–211
    loyalty, 211–212
    trial and repeat, 208–209
Consumer product goods (CPGs), 141
Consumers, 28
    evolution, 138–139
    target, 88, 90, 150
Contingency plan, 198, 217–218
Core qualities of star brands, 2–6
    clarity, 3
    commitment to learning, 5–6
    consistency, 3
    emotional connections, 4
    higher order purpose, 4
    superior benefits, 5
CPGs. See Consumer product goods
Craftsmanship, Harley Davidson equity pyramid, 76–77
CRM. See Customer relationship management
Culliton, James, 166
Customer relationship management (CRM), 147–148

D
Darwin, Charles, 6
Davidson, Harley, equity pyramid, 74–79

Davidson, Walter, 76
Denim Classé jeans brand, 88, 89, 92, 97
Deupree, R. R., 12
Digital media, 146–147
Discovery channel, 65
Discovery communications, 65
Distribution, product, 171, 181–182, 197, 214–215
Dove Camera Shy analysis, 112–115, 132

E
Emotional benefits, brand, 118
Equity
    brand. See Brand equity
    fit, 90–93, 95
Harley Davidson. See Harley Davidson equity pyramid
Equity pyramid, 70–71, 74–79, 89
Executional leadership, 13
Executive summary of document, 193

F
Financial health, 26
Four "Ps," 166, 167
Functional benefits, brand, 118

G
General Motors (GM), 142
Glee, American show, 142
Goals, setting, 8, 45–48, 94, 156
Google's 10X projects, 5
Gordon, Lynne, 123
"Green" brands, 1
Grow: How Ideals Power Growth and Profit at the World's Greatest Companies (Brown), 64
Growth strategy, 50

H
Harley Davidson, marketing planning cycle, 198–200
    Harley Davidson equity pyramid, 74–79
        craftsmanship, 76–77
    HD logo, 78
        110-year heritage, 77
    HOGs, 78–79
        ownable assets, 77–79
        sound, 78
        unique benefits, 76
    V-twin engine technology, 76
Harley Owners Group (HOGs), 78–79
Harley's motorcycles, 77, 78
Harvesting strategy, 51–52

Higher order purpose, 4
HOGs. See Harley Owners Group

I

IBI
  in action, 121–122
  framework, 125
IBM, 65, 66
Idea, 118–121, 127–128, 132–134
In-market testing, 210–211
Insight
  about, 111–112
Dove Camera Shy analysis, 112–115
  false, 116
Sport Club Recife analysis, 115–116
Internal assessment, 22–25
Ivory soap, 12

K

Keller, Kevin Lane, 60
Key performance indicator (KPI) studies, 154, 159

L

Lead with a Story (Smith), 102
Learning organization, 5
Legal regulation, 29
LEGO minifig, 43
Lightning Car, 155–158
Loyalty, 211–212

M

Mad Men magazine, 144
Mahindra & Mahindra, brand target, 82–85
Market assessment, 22, 25–26
Marketing budget, 197–198
Marketing mix, 166–173, 176, 195–196
  placement, 171–172
  price, 172–173
  product, 167–169
  promotion, 169–171
  selection of, 175–184
Marketing mix effectiveness, 206, 212–213
Marketing plan
  and measurement, 9–10
  objective of, 189
  presenting, 201
  process of building, 191
  structure of, 192
  for sustaining strategy, 51

  timeline, 192
  for U.S. Harley Davidson, 198–200
Marketing strategy, 165, 166, 189
  components of, 194–195
  brand equity, 195
  brand target, 195
  communication, 196
  distribution channels, 197
  marketing mix, 195–196
  pricing, 197
  product, 196
  promotional tactics, 196–197
  for sustained growth, 51
Marketing theory, 70
Market mix modeling (MMM), 155
Market sales goal, determination, 156
Market share
  measuring, 206–207
  position, 46–47
Market trends, 28
  consumer, 28
  industry specific, 29–30
  technology, 28–29
Maslow's Hierarchy of Needs, 63, 87, 88, 91, 95
MasterCard, 121
MasterCard Priceless campaign, 133
McElroy, Neil, 12–14
Measurement plan, 198, 203
  steps for building, 203–205
  core metrics selection, 205–215
  data and contingency plan, 217–218
  time period selection, 216–217
Media
  advertising and, 169
  blogger relations, 149
  budgets. See Budgets, media
  CRM, 147–148
  digital, 146–147
  effectiveness, 213–214
  landscape, 138
  out-of-home (OOH), 144–145
  outreach, 148–149
  print, 143–144
  proliferation of, 139
  public relations (PR) and earned, 148–150
  radio, 145–146
  social, 149–150
  technology, 140
  television, 141–142

Media planning, 138
  creating, 150–159
  optimizing each vehicle, 152–153
  right budget level determination, 153–154
  right media vehicles selection, 151–152
  testing, 158–159
  understanding when & where consumer, 150–151
Message
  brand, 176, 178
  effectiveness, 213–214
MMM. See Market mix modeling
Mongrue, Andres, 138
Multicultural marketing, 97
Multi-segment target works, 90

N

Needs based segment, 83–87, 91, 93, 95
New Emerging Market Multinationals: Four Strategies
  for Disrupting Markets and Building Brands, The, 82
Nielsen AdViews, 154, 156
Nike, 1

O

Operational discipline, 14
Opportunities, market, 33
Out-of-home (OOH), 144–145
Ownable brand assets, 72–73, 77–79

P

Packaging, brand, 72
Patagonia, 4
Placement, marketing mix, 171–172
Points of difference, 70, 76, 149
Points of parity, 70
Pre-market testing, 209–210, 214
Price, 180, 197, 215
  marketing mix, 172–173
  promotion incentives, 169–170
Priceless campaign analysis, 122
Print, 143–144
Procter & Gamble (P&G), 4, 12, 14, 64
Product, 167–169
Profit, 47–48, 207–208
Promotion
  incentives, 180–181, 196–197
  marketing mix, 169–171
Protect and defend strategy, 51
Public relations (PR) and earned media, 148–150

R

Radio ads, 145–146
Receptivity, 133, 150
Recognizable brand assets, 77–79
Repeat, brand, 176, 208–209
Return on investment (ROI), 130, 212, 214
Risk management planning, 198, 217–218
ROI. See Return on investment

S

Sales
  brand, 176, 177
  measuring, 206
  ratio, SWOT analysis to adjust, 157
Sales growth, 45–46
  common metrics of, 46
  expectations, 46
Sampling, 170–171
Schultz, Howard, 41
Segmenting market, 82, 85
  brand target, 85–89
Maslow's Hierarchy of Needs, 91
Senge, Peter, 5
Share of voice (SOV), 154
SMART brand goals, 45
"Smarter Planet" campaign, 65, 66
Smith, Paul, 102
Social media, 149–150
SOV. See Share of voice
Spend-to-sales ratio, 156
Sport Club Recife, 114, 115, 132
Star Brand Model, 6–8
  assessment and goal setting, 8
  brand equity and target, 8–9
  communication strategy, 9
  marketing plan and measurement, 9–10
  marketing strategy, 9
  using, 8–10
Starbucks, 1, 40, 41, 72
Stengel, Jim, 4, 64
Strengths, SWOT, 32
Sub-segment strategy, 94–97
Sustain strategy, 50–51
SWOT analysis, 30–34, 157

T

Target
  brand. See Brand target
  consumers, 88, 150

Television commercials, 141–142
Threats, SWOT, 33
Top of mind awareness, 213
Trial, brand, 129, 176, 208–209

U
Uber, 65

V
Vision
  crafting, 40
  critiquing, 44
  setting, 39–40
Volume per customer, 183
V-twin engine technology, 76

W
Walmart, 182
Wanamaker, John, 153
Weaknesses, SWOT, 32

Z
Zappos, 168

A Brief Bio

Carolina Rogoll has been building some of the world's most beloved brands for over ten years. Employed at Procter & Gamble, the world's largest consumer packaged goods company, she has worked across different product categories in global markets and led several complex initiatives with diverse teams. She has passion for building winning brands and a strong track record in business management and coaching.

Dedicated to growing capability, she has been on the faculty of the first-ever Masters in Branding program at the School of Visual Arts in New York City since 2011, where she created the inaugural (and very popular) brand management seminar.

Carolina graduated Magna Cum Laude in Business Administration from Universidad de los Andes, Colombia, South America and Summa Cum Laude with dual undergraduate degrees in Marketing and Management from the A.B. Freeman School of Business, Tulane University in New Orleans, Louisiana. She received her MBA with honors at Williams College of Business, Xavier University in Cincinnati, Ohio. She speaks German, Spanish, Italian, and Portuguese.

Books from Allworth Press

Allworth Press is a division of Skyhorse Publishing, Inc.
Selected titles are listed below.

The Art of Digital Branding, Revised Edition
by Ian Cocoran (6 x 9, 272 pages, paperback, $19.95)

Brand Thinking and Other Noble Pursuits
by Debbie Millman (6 x 9, 320 pages, paperback, $19.95)

Corporate Creativity: Developing an Innovative Organization
by Thomas Lockwood and Thomas Walton (6 x 9, 256 pages, paperback, $24.95)

Effective Leadership for Nonprofit Organizations
by Thomas Wolf (6 x 9, 192 pages, paperback, $16.95)

Emotional Branding, Revised Edition
by Marc Gobe (6 x 9, 344 pages, paperback, $19.95)

From Idea to Exit: The Entrepreneurial Journey
by Jeffrey Weber (6 x 9, 272 pages, paperback, $19.95)

Infectious: How to Connect Deeply and Unleash the Energetic Leader Within
by Achim Nowak (6 x 9, 256 pages, paperback, $19.95)

Intentional Leadership: 12 Lenses for Focusing Strengths, Managing Weaknesses, and Achieving Your Purpose
by Jane A. G. Kise (7 x 10, 200 pages, paperback, $19.95)

Millennial Rules: How to Sell, Serve, Surprise & Stand Out in a Digital World
by T. Scott Gross (6 x 9, 208 pages, paperback, $16.95)

Peak Business Performance Under Pressure
by Bill Driscoll (6 x 9, 224 pages, paperback, $19.95)

The Pocket Small Business Owner's Guide to Building Your Business
by Kevin Devine (5 ½ x 8 ¼, 256 pages, paperback, $14.95)

The Pocket Small Business Owner's Guide to Business Plans
by Brian Hill and Dee Power (5 x 8 , 224 pages, paperback, $14.95)

The Pocket Small Business Owner's Guide to Negotiating
by Kevin Devine (5 ½ x 8 ¼, 224 pages, paperback, $14.95)

Rebuilding the Brand
by Clyde Fessler (6 x 9, 128 pages, paperback, $14.95)

To see our complete catalog or to order online, please visit www.allworth.com.